The Medii

Step into the Mind of a Medium

By Sharon Bengalrose

The Medium's Handbook
Step into the Mind of a Medium
Copyright © 2018 by Sharon Bengalrose Healing
Published by Bengalrose Healing
Designed by Sharon Barbour
Author - Sharon's spirit inspiration writing team
Book cover illustration – by Chris from
www.cimbart.co.uk

Printed in the United Kingdom

ISBN-13: 978-1718630505
ISBN- -10: 1718630506

Welcome

We welcome you to 'The Medium's Handbook - Step into the Mind of a Medium'. The fact you have this book in your hands tells us you are aware that you have gifts capable of connecting to the spirit realm, or you have been lead to teaching mediumship. Please accept that part of your life's mission is discovering your true life's purpose – and to be an advocate for the spirit realm.

We have come together to provide a book that will guide you on the spiritual journey you are about to undertake. We have stepped into the mind of our medium friend who we channel through and gathered true knowledge of their journey, plus examples to help guide you on yours. This book is based on experiences of a human who has already taken the journey, what they discovered, and what they learnt. We will give you the tools to take your journey towards mediumship and healing; imagine this book is your handbook of guidance.

Many of you taking this journey will be guided to become spiritual teachers and advocates for the spirit realm in the future. So we have included some teaching exercises to inspire the teachers amongst you, but also to inspire you, the student and what to expect when you learn on this journey.

Now let us step into your mind and enjoy the journey!

CONTENTS

Welcome

Section 1

What is a medium?

The simple answer to the question, 'What is a medium?' is that it is the practice of humans, known as mediums, who mediate communication between spirits of the dead and living human beings. Now as you can imagine, there is a lot more to it than that.

After working with many Earth mediums over the years, we feel the starting point for any medium or healer is to understand the basic energies of Mother Earth and the universe. Our chosen medium friend for this book worked with us for a few years before we realised this would help her understand how and why their own human energies varied. These variations depended on what aspect of work they were doing, whether it was living everyday lives, spiritual healing or mediumship.

So we need to start by explaining the energy of our universe and how it affects the spirit realm and the Earth in different ways. This involves the physical makeup of the universe and the energy of thought.

When a human is born, they are born fully open to unconditional love; they see, hear, feel and sense the spirit realm as well as other ascension beings. Within you is your soul, or as we like to call it, the spirit within. Your soul has a connection to your higher self in the spirit

1

realm and your soul is here to learn but also to guide you on your life's path to a better way of being. Now a lot of humanity will live their lives unaware of this connection. But there are those amongst you who have chosen to work in the higher, lighter love energy, who are known amongst you as light workers – a medium or healer are two examples. As you study mediumship you will come to realise that some of you will use the gifts you are born with from a young age, while for others, the gifts come to them later in life. Some have a powerful connection without much study, while others need to work at it. The reason for these differences are the chosen lessons to be learnt while on this mediumship path on Mother Earth.

The spirit within you, which some of you know as the 'Soul', is made up of a multidimensional energy, a living being with highly ascended telepathic mind powers, existing in a high frequency energy plane of unconditional love and light. The spirit within exists out of time and space in what we can best describe as the NOW moment. For humanity's understanding we describe our spirit realm as the fifth energy dimension, and we also have further higher dimension levels within our ascension hierarchy.

Every frequency level of energy in the third, fourth and fifth dimensions and beyond, has its own reality, to which your multidimensional self can adapt. As you move through the different levels, your consciousness adapts and raises its frequency to that reality.

Humanity lives in the **third dimension physical lower frequency energy dimension,** known as the third dimension physical self. Within the third dimension is also what we call a third dimension matrix, the aim of which is to hold the spirit within in place, and controls the human and spirit within connection while they are joined on earth. This means the human will not remember the previous existences of the spirit within or its memories, unless they have chosen to do so for their spiritual path. The challenge has been for the spirit within to be the student, learning and fulfilling an Earth mission. While doing this, they try to bring more love and light to your world. Their aim is to trigger in the human a better way of living and existence without the human having prior knowledge of this. One day humanity will be like us, and also have the abilities to aid other worlds, realms and dimensions and be the spirit within. Our soul connection will no longer be needed as humanity will have ascended and will be living in unconditional love energy alongside us in thought and practice, while still living on Earth. Further on in the future humans will have the choice to keep the physical body or live in the conscious state of being if you reach a high ascension level.

At the moment the third dimension is a busy, chattering dimension full of fear, anger and feelings of powerlessness, and you feel lost in the world you live in. You feel you want to do more for your world, but you are swimming against a heavy current, living in hope the tide will change and the world will know peace. When you start on the spiritual journey, you begin to raise your vibration, and this will change how you see and feel about your third dimensional world.

In this dimension, you can create your reality through your own mind restrictions – hate attracting hate, love attracting love, a circle of events that keeps repeating the same pattern unless you can see the light of a higher existence. You can change your reality by moving your attention to other things – your reality is where your mind is in that moment of your time. For example, if you watched the news and saw the biggest massacre shooting in the USA, your mind would be connecting with the fear, anger and confusion of your world and you stay in that spiral of feelings. If you turn your attention to a walk in a beautiful forest and the love you have for your family, you experience kindness, love and peace instead of fear. I hope this helps you understand this. If you change your reality as you see it, this will raise your energy. You attract more of the reality your attention is focused on, hate-to-hate, or love-to-love. These emotions also affect your physical body and its powers to self-heal and ascend, keeping you in the time and space of the third dimension reality.

The fourth energy dimension we call the fourth dimension astral self. This is what we call the middle ground, the stepping-stone to the fifth dimension. The fourth dimension is an astral plane that is smoother flowing, offering possibility and capabilities, with more clarity of the universe and with that, more hope for humanity. You will find this astral plane while in your dreams and the meditation state of being. Have you heard of astral travel while in your dream state? We use this fourth dimension conscious state of being to give you guidance and messages. Because of rigid third dimension energy, many of you will forget about these on awakening, or just after, so it is key to record any unusual dreams. For those of you that have started to raise your vibration, you will remember more of the dreams and visualisations in meditation, but you should still record these as over time, they could fade.

This fourth dimension astral energy plane leads you away from the hate and anger energy towards the love energy, which prepares you for the unconditional love energy of the fifth dimension. To enter the fourth dimension astral plane you need to raise your state of consciousness by working in the thoughts of peace, love and light. Some of you are starting to work in this energy dimension with the shift since your Earth year 2000. Since around 2012, this shift has accelerated and there are notable changes in humanity, with its attitude moving more towards the spiritual way of being. The more of you that lift your vibration, the more of you will be transported to the fourth dimension way of thinking and being. Your attention will shift to the thinking pattern needed to ascend into the fifth dimension reality and with this, your Earth will become more enlightened and the shift will really begin to move along at a fast pace.

The fifth high frequency energy dimension is a high frequency energy plane that exists in a permanent state of peace, bliss, love, kindness and joy. We like to think of this version of you as the light body self. We have no time or space restraints, we exist in the here and now in unity, with no worries about past or future. No more negative thoughts stream into the mind of a being that has reached fifth dimension consciousness. Your mind is quieter, allowing for telepathic skills and conscious growth; you will be without the constant chatter that flows into the third dimension mind. While in this wonderful fifth dimension, you can also connect to the universe knowledge pot and so much more. Humanity can exist at this level on Earth, in your human form, if you lose your layers of doubt, worry, anger and fear.

As you develop you will hear others talk of the veil - the divide between the fifth dimension and the third dimension. When we wish to communicate with a human we have to drop down towards the third energy plane and to get a good connection and a medium has to raise their energies to meet ours. Developing is all about building this power within you – think of it as a muscle that needs strengthening. When she teaches, our medium friend describes it as building a muscle, and eventually you achieve a six-pack! She brings humour and says you never stop learning – she is a three-pack aiming to be a full six-pack one day. What we love is that, by letting go of the ego, she has recognised she will never stop learning on this mediumship path.

What is mediumship?

On Earth, you will see the terms spiritual, medium, clairvoyant and psychic. The individual may use the terms to describe a psychic medium, a clairvoyant medium or psychic clairvoyant medium. We wish you to understand the difference.

A psychic receives information about events and people from the vibration energy of a person, place, or object. A psychic can read a person's energy and may perceive past and present events, or even seem to project future events in that person's life; some may also connect on a clairvoyant level. They will see this in their mind's eye and feel energy and emotion to build their reading. They are working more in the three-dimensional energy level, but also at times linking into guided information from a higher frequency. Now, when you work at this level, trust that your guides and your client's guides are helping to bring the positive guidance and information needed for their client to continue forward on their life's journey. They do this telepathically mind-to-mind and soul-to-soul.

A medium communicates directly from their mind (mental mediumship) with spirits of those no longer living. To do this they have to raise their energies above the third dimensional energy planes to a half-way point that enables them to meet with the spirit coming in from the fifth dimensional energy. When this happens the medium and spirits are drawing on their own energies and those around them to help achieve this. If you ever have a reading with a medium and you feel a pull on your sola plexus in the stomach area, this is the energy exchange. Mental mediumship takes place when you communicate with spirits while fully conscious. As the word mental denotes, this form of mediumship uses the mind – the intuitive mind, not the rational or logical part. They do this telepathically mind-to-mind and soul-to-soul. Now we say soul-to-soul – your spirit within – because when you connect with us there is a deeper level of connection than mind-to-mind. The communicating spirit connects with the medium's spirit within at a unconditional love energy level. Then the medium's spirit within connects with the recipient of the message, creating a triangle of deep soul connection all linking together to help the mind links, and working as a team to create the needed healing and messages.

A clairvoyant is someone with the ability to experience in a visual way what they can clearly see with their mind's eye, also known as the third eye. You can see how the name can then be linked with both mediums and psychics, as these people will be clairvoyant with clear visual seeing, on both the psychic link and the medium higher energy link.

The aim of all psychics or mediums should be to bring the two worlds of spirit and Earth plane closer together, allowing you to connect with your loved ones or give the loving healing messages and guidance that is needed. We do see mediums start off on a psychic link before they link clairvoyantly. Others will reach the clairvoyant link straight away. It is a team effort between them and us and it is a case of finding what is best for that medium, linking their thought process and energy to how they work. Whatever your age, when you start your journey with us we have to learn to work with you in the best way we can. This will be by finding your strengths, and what you will become − a psychic, a medium, or perhaps a spiritual healer. Remember you are all unique, so it is very important to us that you are comfortable with the way you work with us.

For us to connect with you, we have to step into a person's mind by the way of telepathic thought. We have learnt to adjust from our fifth high frequency energy dimension to filter our thoughts through your denser third dimension physical mind. Learning to raise your energies is also a great help to us. All spirits and Earth beings have individual energy signatures so every time we link with a human we have to adjust and treat it as a new experience, as no two humans or spirits are ever the same. When we connect with you we use the information sitting in your brain from your life experiences. This is a team effort, as we give you the thoughts of the dead person trying to connect, and you then have to interpret them. Once you have done this, you have to TRUST to give out the information you have received. You then relay this to your client, working as team with them. If they cannot take in everything you say, you come back to us to clarify, which is why it's a team effort and such a key part of your success.

This type of mental mediumship falls into several distinct types, which are described below for you:

Clairsentience – (clear feeling) Perceiving information by way of strong, emphatic feelings and emotions from spirit. For example - how did they feel on their passing, what type of personality did they have, were they happy or miserable!

Clairvoyant – (vision) Seeing with the mind's eye objects, colours, symbols, people, spirits or scenes. These pictures are not visible to the naked eye and usually flash into the medium's mind. This can feel as if it's being projected in front of you and you see a vision.

Clairaudient – (hearing) Perceiving [sensing and picking up] sounds or words from sources broadcasting from a spiritual realm. Now don't get confused – most of you will hear our thoughts within your mind, but a few of you will hear the spirit voice as if a fellow human is standing next to you and talking in your ear.

Clairempathy – (emotion) Sensing or feeling within one's self the attitude or emotions of another person. This is a deeper level than Clairsentience; you will really take on the person's personality, and the emotions of that lifetime.

Clairgustance – (tasting") Discerning the essence of a substance through taste from spirit. A good example is the taste of smoking, a drink they liked or a distinctive flavour such as garlic.

Clairscent – (smelling). Detecting a fragrance or odour coming from the spirit. This is very popular way for spirits to express themselves through, for example, a grandma's favourite perfume or flower, or again, cigarette or cigar smoke.

Clairtangency – (touching) This ability is commonly known as Psychometry. By holding an object or touching an area, you perceive information about the article, its owner or history through the palms of your hands. This is more on the Psychic level.

Now, what have you noticed about the various ways we can work with you in your mediumship? It should be apparent that we can work with all of your senses. When we step into the medium's mind with our thoughts, the human brain has control of your body and the signals needed for the human to recognise, smell, taste, touch etc; we simply connect with these. As we learn to work with the medium we will trigger the senses that individual best responds to. It's rare for a medium to use all of these; quite often, one or two stand out at first, and as they build their mediumship muscle, we add a couple of others. Our medium friend is a Clairvoyant, Clairsentience and Clairempathy, which were the strongest connections we found as she was developing. She is also a very creative visual person, so a vision was easy for her to understand. We have just started introducing Clairtangency to our medium friend, which is interesting for us to observe; we started by giving her the taste of tea, so she knows her spirit connection loved tea. We have to experiment to see what works for you as an individual, and build on the successes or try something new.

As your mediumship develops you will recognise these abilities in your work; as we've said, it's unlikely you will have all of them – the average is about four per medium – and we aim to find with each individual the best way for you to use your mind and senses with us.

We would also like to take this opportunity to tell you about other forms of mediumship.

Trance mediumship - There are many different 'Levels' and depths of trance, between the state of 'Light Trance' where the medium is still aware of the room they are in and what is going on around them. In the lighter levels the medium is inspired and get deeper as they progress on the trance journey. 'Deep Trance', is where a medium can be totally unconscious and unaware of anything that is happening within themselves and around them. Some can have awareness but feel very distant from their normal reality. All levels is what we would call an altered state of being with different degrees of awareness.

With most mediums it can take years to develop the trance mediumship. 'It would be unusual if a medium would be able to go into deep trance and bring through the communicator in the communicator's voice and mannerisms first time of sitting. The early days are spent in what we would call a lighter trance level where you will speak the words of the communicator, and slowly developing into deeper trance, where the personalities and transfiguring can take place. We must make this clear to remove the fear that some of you think we enter your body, because we do not. We connect with your individual energy field and mind as we do with, say, clairvoyant mediumship; you learn to trust and let go so our thoughts and words can come through for you to speak. As you develop your trance, you will go deeper and this allows us to build a voice box so it sounds like the spirit communicator, then more of the personality will come forth, and we can place an energy veil over your face (over shadowing) to alter it to look like the communicator to the human eye. We find trance helps mediums with their connection to spirit. Most mediums that sit in a trance circle will become better mediums as it helps to build their clairvoyant connection.

If you are drawn to trance, we advise you sit in a closed circle to develop. This is so that the same people commit to each time of meeting, so your energies can blend and we can learn to work with you all and build the energy in the circle to help each individual develop. A trance circle will be headed up by a trance teacher that will observe each session but not enter the trance state themselves. It is important you have an experienced trance teacher, so they can explain each stage of the journey to you and what you are experiencing. They are to function under prayer, asking for protection and always to set the intent of the evening's trance session. We feel it is important you do not try to develop on your own as we recommend an observer. If you think about spirit wanting to come and communicate to help humanity, who will hear our words if you do this on your own?

Once you have sat in a trance circle and understand the way it works, we would feel OK about you trying inspirational writing at home, asking a guide to step forward to give you inspirational words. We do see this used in mediumship development groups now, as it is a great way to build your trust and confidence in your guide's connection. A lot of books have been channeled to Earth by this method. This can be through handwriting or if the trance state is strong enough, mind-to-mind straight to the computer keyboard. You can also sit and ask your trance guides to come and be with you, to attune and adjust your energies when you are more experienced. We ask you to always open and close in prayer and clearly state your intent. Our medium friend has been able to channel our words through her trance and commitment to it. We are guiding more and more developing mediums to sit in trance as we have found it really builds a strong connection with the spirit realm and Trust.

We would also like to mention trance healing, as it is a very powerful method, with the healing energies coming directly from spirit. With spiritual beings so much closer to your energy, this form of healing can work at a deeper level. Trance healing works on emotional and spiritual issues more than physical issues but is not the only rule. If physical issues are attached to emotional and spiritual issues then all elements may be addressed. Spiritual/psychic surgery may be performed as directed by spirit. Our medium friend now works in the trance healing method. As we have said previously, Reiki healing connects to your healing guides, but the trance healing is a deeper connection with them. You will feel and see your guides there with you. Our friend has an Indian chief called White Cloud who comes in on trance healing, he has big hands and our medium friend can feel this as the healing starts.

Quite often a physical medium is discovered when they start to sit in trance circles or workshops.

A physical medium is capable of producing physical phenomena that are either felt or seen by others in the same room as we, the external spirit entities, manipulate the energies and substances of the medium. These phenomena can be in the form of etheric energy-matter known as ectoplasm, materialisation of spirit, breezes, rapping noises, spirit voices, lights or moving objects.

They may also produce an apport object – a physical object that appears in a room or other enclosed space into which orthodox entry is impossible. The apport has to pass through matter to the space it arrives in.

There is also something called transfiguration, where the face of a spirit person can be seen forming over the medium's face. For best results this is done in a red light so the energy veil can form over the sitters' faces without being destroyed. There will be varied results where faces can be very clear at times, with the medium's face completely disappearing. At other times you may see many faces that can appear over a medium's face quite rapidly, but each one is distinct from the other. You will see features like beards and moustaches and objects like glasses or earrings and head wear. The hair and body shape can alter, such as the length or thickness of fingers. The events listed here can also occur in more advanced trance circles.

Another area we work on with the medium is direct voice, where the voice of a spirit speaks to sitters out of mid-air. The voices are created from an artificial voice box formed from ectoplasm taken from the physical medium. We use the psychic power which is generated from the sitters to help form ectoplasm for the communication so some music is played and singing helps bring the energy power up. Once the power is sufficient it can take a few minutes for a spirit to master the voice box. Once the voices come through it's as clear and powerful as anyone talking in the room. You can often ask questions and the answers can be made from the spirit individual communicators.

Although this is fascinating, many of you might never witness a physical medium as they are mainly in closed circles. The circle is made up of a select few, which support the physical medium with their energy and make sure they stay safe. The drawback to doing physical mediumship is that it can be tremendously draining on the medium's body as it uses their energy and has an effect on their physical body and health. We are continuously working in the spirit realm to find ways to connect and control the energies so the human form is not as affected by our connection to them. This is because this can affect their physical makeup and health over the years.

Some of you might not even be aware of physical mediums, as even in your modern day and freethinking in the western world it is kept behind closed doors. Circles have declined as it takes time, patience and dedication from the medium and circle sitters, and the modern day fast pace of life conflicts with this. Sometimes circle members have to leave, which breaks the energy bond built up, and can slow the developing physical medium's progress. We also might ask a circle member to leave if their energy is not right at that time.

We actually asked our medium friend to leave the physical

circle she sat in, as the physical medium's energy was conflicting with hers. It was actually to help our medium friend fulfil her potential. Since then, the foresaid circle has had more changes, as we find the right people and balance. But it is important the physical circles are closed for protection to the sitter and for us to build the energies and connection with the support sitters. Those in the know will get to see this phenomenon over time, when the circle chooses to open its doors to a demonstration or the sitter is guided to travel with this to different Earth places.

There are a lot of books on the subject in your world. It you are drawn to find out more then we suggest you connect to a physical circle and they can advise further on how they work and give guidance on the subject.

Section 2

How do you become a medium?

You all start your journey towards becoming a medium in various ways. Our medium friend started her journey by general spiritual experiences through her life. We also gave her a repetitive memory as a dream from one of her previous lives. This is what opened the door for us; her curiosity led her to have a past life regression, which sparked her interest in the spirit realm and so her spiritual journey really began. Many of you start your spiritual journey by being guided to using your healing gifts and do Reiki healing which we brought to earth to aid humanity. Reiki is a form of alternative medicine discovered in 1922 by Japanese Buddhist Mikao Usui. Reiki healers use a technique called palm healing or hands-on healing, through which we can channel our healing energy to the human receiving it. The reason Reiki can be a starting point to mediumship is that it helps clears your energy; you have to deal with any fear, grief or pain that's been holding you back in your life. Once you are attuned, it opens you up as a free-flowing vessel for our unconditional love healing energy. This then leads some of you to feeling your guides and hearing messages in your thoughts from spirit friends and relatives who have passed over, hence leading to an interest in mediumship.

However your life journey unfolds on the mediumship

path, being a medium comes with great responsibility. With this role you are a healer, counsellor and confidant to the person you are reading. You bring the receiver of your messages great comfort and upliftment, bringing the unconditional love energy healing their heart's need.

So, taking the next steps forward to being a practicing medium means accepting the many responsibilities that go with it. You will find yourself close up with a client giving an intimate reading; it is a privilege and honour to be able to share in these very precious and tender moments. Or you might find yourself in front of 100 people, delivering messages that are needed for some in the audience to hear on that day. Either way, remember your message will bring healing, closure and guidance to help them move forward on their life paths with our guidance.

If you want to work as a medium you have a responsibility to make sure you learn your trade in the correct manner, which involves training and learning to practice in a safe way. Part of this is how to conduct yourself and how to deliver messages in a correct manner or tone for that individual or audience. You must respect the three-way triangle – yourself, the receiver of the message, and spirit.

What was your spirit lightbulb moment?

Everyone is born open to spirit, with a connection to the divine. On Earth, we often see that by the age of five, children's ability to connect to us and beyond is shut down, and this has been their chosen path. Some will stay like this, living out their life lessons, but others will at some point have the spirit lightbulb moment and start on their spiritual mediumship or healing path.

Because you're reading this book, you have probably had a lightbulb moment, and we are now guiding you on how to build on this moment you experienced. The starting point is to seek out teachers that are well known in the spiritual circles to develop a safe spiritual path, in prayer and love. It is important to us that we lead you to the correct place to learn, a sanctuary for spiritualism. When you find the correct place you will know it in your heart and you will be welcomed; the like-minded people there will only have good in their hearts for you. When you find the right place, you will then develop on your pathway in whatever direction it is for you to take and believe me, we know what that direction is – it's just your task to discover it.

Please ask for guidance to be led to the right teacher; we will give you signs to help you and as you work to build your connection they will become clearer. Our medium friend was guided to a wonderful lady who ran a Spiritualist Centre in her area, she went one night to an open mediumship development circle – and the next stage of her spiritual journey could really begin. She found it quite funny that we had guided her to a spiritual centre that was based in a horse-stable business in a converted barn. She is allergic to horses, which she discovered when she was learning to ride at the age of seventeen! There were two ways this could have gone for us: her ego could have stepped in and said, 'stay away from the horses to protect yourself', or, as we hoped, she could see this as a sign she was in the right place. Fortunately, it was the latter – she felt very at home at this centre and was made very welcome and knew in her heart it was the right place for her development.

Protection is key for your safe development

Once you decide to take the mediumship path, one of the first things you need to learn about is protection.

You all have a soul in your physical body, a spirit within that is energy that glows like a bright flame. We have the ability to see the inner flame within you all. When you take the step to become a medium or healer your inner light will become brighter. The reason for this is that as you develop, the three-dimensional energy breaks down, raising you towards the fifth dimension energy. You become a brighter beacon in the darker, more restricted three-dimensional energy matrix.

The reason we want to mention protection is not to cause you any fear, but to instill a commonsense approach when you work with unseen energies. You would wear a life jacket if you were out on a boat, so think of your guides as your life jacket – we are here to protect you. You are always in control of your mediumship and from day one must set the rules. You must work in prayer of the conditional love of the divine, asking your guides and angels to protect you at all times.

There are spirits that have not gone to the light. The reasons for this can vary and they seek comfort and can attach themselves to physical beings – humans. Following a sudden death, some spirits are confused; they don't realise they are dead and want to get close to a living person. In these cases, they are often trying to contact the living for help. These attachments might be deliberate or happen without the spirit realising what it's doing. The spirits don't usually have any intention of harming the person they are attached to or trying to contact. There are mediums among you who work to release these spirits back to the light. The spirit realm is aware of these spirits that have not returned to us and we monitor them while trying to guide them home. We would like to take this opportunity to thank the mediums who help us with this work.

We also know there are those of you who believe in evil spirits, and we would like to stress here that there is no evil and no evil spirits. Evil is an Earth word conjured by fear of what humanity does not understand. There are energy fields around Earth that hold beings unseen like the elementals. There are dimensions that hold beings mostly ascended and living in peace. There is a lot humanity does not see, and a glimpse of the unknown can bring fear. We can assure you that we are here to protect Mother Earth and work with other ascended beings for this purpose alone. As humanity ascends your fear-based existence will vanish and you will have a greater understanding of the universe around you.

Your thought process is very important in your daily lives and mediumship work to help aid your protection, and your minds are much more powerful than you realise. Most mediums are empaths, they are sensitive to feelings and your purer energy is more sensitive to negative energy attacks. When someone sends a negative thought energy with the conscious or unconscious intention to inflict harm upon a person, their life, or their family, we call this a psychic attack. Harm can be launched towards the emotional, physical, spiritual, or mental state of a person. The human ego is there for your survival, and because of ego, humans experience jealousy when they see others doing well or they think they are taking their livelihood away from them. It's in these situations where we find the human negative thought energy can be strong and projected towards certain individuals. Some will mean to cause harm, while others may not realise the strength of their own negative thoughts and how they can hurt another being.

Beware of your own thoughts as you start this

mediumship journey. If you feel a pang of jealousy – for example, if a fellow student is advancing quicker than you – learn to recognise this and send love and light to that person. Trust in the journey, your unique individual journey, and you will be fine. You will all develop at different paces and take different paths in your mediumship, so relax and enjoy it.

Every time you work open up in prayer; set the intent with your guides for the type of work you will be doing and desired outcome – always ask for the highest and the best. When you finish, thank your guides and spirit for working with you. We give you an example below of how no protection can affect you and your health.

When she was first interested in being a medium, our medium friend was led to a mediumship workshop. The workshop teaching was on a psychic level, building to a clairvoyant mind-to-mind mediumship level with the help of the teacher medium. The teaching medium neglected to instruct the class about shutting down their energies and protection in prayer. In some ways, this helped us see what our medium friend would hear, feel and see, but also it worked against us, as she was a bit fearful of the next experiences she encountered. She started to hear voices in the house at night, see shadow figures, and in bed at night, she felt as if spirit was queuing up in the bedroom to see her. Her energies started to drop as she was open to spirit all the time and she got very tired. We thought it best she got some guidance, and led her back to her Reiki

Master who told her that she needed to shut down to them and helped her to understand the importance of self-protection and taking control. We know this stopped her connection with spirit for a while, but it was more important to protect the chosen Earth being so we could complete our mission with her.

The positive outcome was that when she started up again in mediumship development she made sure it was done with protection and within a proper development circle before she went out on her own. This was also a great lesson for future teaching – understanding the importance of preserving your human energies.

Grounding and protecting your energy's

It is important to do something called grounding on a daily or regular basis; this can be done through simple meditation and your own thought process. When working with spirit your energies will be running on a higher level to Mother Earth's three-dimensional Earth plane. This can affect your human energy levels and make you tired, or out of sorts. So it is important to bring yourself back to connect with Mother Earth often so your energies stay balanced. A tired medium is not a good medium; here is a simple meditation technique to help you.

This can be used anywhere, walking your dog, sitting in the garden, in work, or after you have worked with spirit and healing. (Note: not when you are driving or working machinery). Grounding helps you be focused and calm, it keeps you in the right energy vibration to deal with your daily life.

Below is a simple grounding technique to help you with this:

Grounding technique

Sitting in a chair make sure your feet are on the ground, or on a cushion if legs are short.

Now close your eyes.

Take your mind to the base of the spine; be aware of it on the chair seat.

Now take your mind to the soles of your feet; imagine the base of your feet, feel them in your shoes or on the floor, feel the sensation of skin rubbing the floors or shoes.

Now take you mind back to the base of your spine again. Imagine there are roots growing down towards Mother Earth and pass your feet into the soil.

Now take your attention to the soles of your feet, imagine roots growing from them joining the spine roots, mixing and intertwining in to Mother Earth soil.

Your roots are growing and going deeper and deeper into Mother Earth, they reach the beautiful layers of crystals, with amazing colours shining and sparkling, they are shining out positive energy, wrap your roots around and around these crystals.

Now your roots keep growing and you reach the golden core of Mother Earth's love. Here you are safe and surrounded by love. Wrap your roots around her golden core feeling her healing energy. Now your roots will stay wrapped around Mother Earth keeping you calm and safe.

Open your eyes when you feel ready.

Another method our medium friend chooses to use is a bubble of protection. She does this when she does readings and platform, or is sensing bad vibes around her. She asks her guide and angels to protect her. Now just be aware when you choose to place yourself in protection, as your thought and intent is what will be received and created for you. The protection balance should be a meshed bubble in thought, that lets no harmful energies into your energy field and mind. But it should be set in a way that your mind could send out thoughts to your guides and spirit friends when you give readings and healing. Your guides will be the ones helping to protect you and understand what is needed, but they are guided by your own feelings and fears while on this mediumship journey. Our medium friend has learnt to trust she is protected, and at times when she has been vulnerable to psychic attacks she asks for help. This is because with her experience she has learnt to understand her own energies and know when something is wrong.

Opening and closing your energies

When you work as a medium you open up your energies,

remember the light flame. When you finish a reading or platform you need to shut yourself down. This is because if you walk around open connecting to spirit all day, it drains your energies and can make you ill.

To close down after each time you work is simple. Set the intention with your guides after each time you work, close in prayer and shut down. Then set the intention when you open in your mind in prayer you open up. Our medium friend does this; it now happens without her thinking about it, she trusts us and has mutual respect for us as we have for her, and now it is as she wishes to work.

Sitting in the silence building your inner power

As we have developed our links with mediums over the years, we have found they strengthen their links with us when they are aware of their own various energies and those around them. This starts by them getting to know their own body energy pattern well, then learning how to connect with the spirit realm's unconditional love powerful energy. This will then lead them to recognising the energy of their guides and other spiritual beings that wish to connect. The purpose of sitting in the power is to develop an awareness of energies arising from these different sources and understand how those energies may affect our own energy power levels during the blending process. This also helps with your connection at a deeper level with your soul the spirit within, remember the triangle of soul connection that helps with the readings.

Here is an exercise to help you achieve this:

Note - If your find your mind wandering when doing this exercise, just take your awareness back to your breath and continue where you left off. It doesn't matter how many times your mind wanders as practice will help this, and this exercise helps to build the ability to hold your focus.

Find a quite peaceful space where you cannot be disturbed.

Sitting upright, close your eyes and gently take your awareness to your breath.

Be aware of your breath as you breathe in... and... out...

Do this a few times until you notice yourself starting to relax.

On your next 'in' breath, imagine your power or light within, imagine that slowly expanding on every 'in' breath. Expand your inner light so it fills your whole body.

Continue with this until you imagine you're filling the room with your power.

Continue with the 'in' breath, and imagine this power expanding out into nature, around Mother Earth, and finally progress and imagine this power expanding out into the universe until you reach the spirit realm of unconditional love.

Stay with this power, taking notice of how this unconditional love power is affecting you. This can be physically, mentally or emotionally, or all three at once.

When you have sat in their wonderful energy for a while mentally send an invitation out to the spirit realm consciousness for this power to now blend with your power. Take notice of how this affects you again

When you are ready bring yourself back into your space and normal consciousness. Don't rush. Take your time and have a lovely glass of cool water waiting for your return.

Now as your power builds, remember the mediumship muscle, you then can feel the differentiation between energies better and help build the connection with spirit.

Knowledge is key

When we connect with your energy and spirit within, our thought energy steps into your mind, and the message to the recipient has to be given from the knowledge and memories of this lifetime you are in now. For example: Our medium friend's father in-law loved old cars, read magazines on the subject and owned an old green Ford Prefect. She was doing a reading and was connected to someone's relative and we clairvoyantly showed her these memories, the green Ford and a pile of magazines. She then said, "I have a man here who loved old cars and reading about the subject". She kept it simple, as their relative might have had an old red car and lots of books on it. But with her memory and their memories of their loved one we made the connection and bought forward the evidence. Once you have that connection, you could ask us to show the colour say of the car – we can build on that first thought. You have to trust what is being shown you and learn how to decipher it.

So based on this, we advise you to gain knowledge outside your own memories, watch documentaries, antique and travel programmes, read about the world around you and the more you have stored in your mind the more we can use. This can be done outside of workshops and development groups. We also advise you read spiritual books, as we will guide you to the right ones for you on your journey – you could learn about angels, or shamanic healing, whatever you are drawn to, take a leap of trust and buy it or borrow it.

Development circles and works shops

We would ask you to seek out an open development circle for mental mediumship as you start your mediumship journey. Open circle means that each time the circle meets, it will vary depending on who's there. The open circle will most likely have a mix of beginners and those who have sat in the circle for a few years. As you advance you could then find a closed circle. A closed circle has a select number and high commitment is required so the energies of the circle each time they meet are the same. This helps us build the power within you and strengthens our connection, thus aiding your development. In any circle the teacher will provide exercises to do each week to help with your development. The teacher will draw on their own experiences with the help of their guides.

When you find your circle we ask, my friends, that you never compare yourself to others; instead learn from them all, as they will from you. We see many potential mediums stop at this early stage because they doubt their abilities. You are all unique and individual; your guides will use these development opportunities to find the best way of working with you as an individual and you will all develop at different stages.

If you do not know of any development circles, visit your local spiritualist churches and ask around, or try a Mind and Body fair. We will guide you to where you need to be but you need to put in the groundwork too. We recommend you sit in one circle if you're a beginner, but as you really start to develop you might be led to another circle, or a second circle. You will be guided to what you need for your own unique journey.

Another development method is workshops for developing mediums. We see these as very useful tools as you have five to six hours of tuition and being with like minded people learning. Remember you all learn from each other on this journey.

Some mediums run extended workshops that then give you certificates to be a practicing medium. We would like to say for the new developing mediums there is not right or wrong way to learn your trade. If we put ten practicing mediums plucked from your various societies in a room, they will all have a unique story to tell you of how they developed to be a medium. There are various teaching methods and there are various unique human characters. You will learn in an environment that suits you, remember you cannot fit a square peg in to around hole. The end result we seek with all teaching methods is a medium that works from their heart, connecting to their spirit within and giving out unconditional love and light energy in messages. To achieve this you need to release the EGO, as this is what prevents you achieving this.

Make sure you are covered

When you choose to take your gifts out to others, such as readings or healing in your own home, or public domain, you must make sure you are covered for liability. The law in some of your lands demands this. The misunderstanding over the centuries of healers and humans with the gift was misunderstood and feared, and the Witches Act came about because of this. The laws have altered over the years. Our medium friend is based in the United Kingdom and the law says she has to be insured and display or state a disclaimer.

Because of this, make sure you have a disclaimer when practicing your gifts. We provide a simple one below, or you can have something more detailed.

Please note that all demonstrations and readings are for educational, experimental and entertainment purposes only.

Depending on where you live in your world, please check the legal law of your country and work within these diameters, this could include insurance and a disclaimer.

Section 3

Spirit Guides

Every human has a group of spirits from our realm that will be with you throughout your life for guidance and protection. It was decided a long time ago that every physical being we were with would have a guide that would accompany the spirit within while in a physical form from birth to death. Some of you call this guide a Gatekeeper – the main spirit guide that guides your entry to this life and return back home. These Gatekeeper guides have wide-ranging experience, and will have undertaken various lives as spirit within, giving them a deep understanding of any problems that might arise; alongside the deep wisdom they have gained from their life experiences. There are two additional guides there to support the main guide; their role is to run errands back to the spirit realm, source information as needed, and give healing. Depending on their experience, they may also use their own learning as guidance to the spirit within and yourself. Other guides will join you on your life's journey, dictated by major factors on your life path when there are important changes in your life – motherhood, education, health and spiritual development are just a few examples. So you have the same three guides with you all the time, and others coming and going as needed.

A lot of humanity will be unaware of changing guides, but those of you that have opened to spirit and have an understanding of their own energies will sense when this happens. As one guide leaves and another joins you, it causes an energy dip and the new guide has to adjust to your energy field before they can work with you properly, and this can take a few of your Earth days to happen. As well as guides, you will have at least two guardian angels; these are from our realm in the higher ascended levels; they have not had a physical body spirit within experience so their energy is purer and on a higher frequency. They will be with you to watch over you, offer protection and give healing when called upon by you and us. You are aware of some of the highly ranked guardian angels such as Archangel Michael, but there are thousands more all serving humanity and other worlds.

You have other guides as well; animal guides from the animal kingdom and also some of your guides could be high-ascended star beings. Our star being friends help has increased in the last seventy years since world war two to help the Earth energies rise. They have collaborated with us for a long time to help the universe, and more races of these beings have been coming forward to help and monitor your Mother Earth.

Now key to your development as a medium is building your connection with your guides and recognising their energies. There are some simple practices to help aid this. These can be done in development circles. The first one here could be practiced on your own, once you have developed your habit of working in prayer and protection (see section 2).

Exercise 1 - Connecting with your guides

Sit in a quiet room where you will not be disturbed. Open in prayer and set the intent you are asking to work with a chosen guide so you can feel their energies as they blend with your energy field.

Now sit in the silence and notice how your own body feels, scan yourself from head to foot. It's important you get to know your physical body and any sensations you feel as YOU. When you feel confident you know your own body energy, ask for the chosen guide to work with you on this exercise to step forward into your energy field. Take time to observe any changes – common ones are temperature changes. You might feel pressure over the third eye, tingling on your head, or somewhere on your body. You might even smell an odour or have a sudden small vision. You might just sense someone next to you or in the room. Acknowledge in your mind what you sense so we know what you have felt. Then ask for the guide to step right back out of your energy.

Take time to observe how you feel now they have left your energy field. Now ask the chosen guide to step back into your energy closer than before, as close as they can. Observe again how you feel. The sensations from the first time might intensify or you might experience something new. Again, acknowledge in your mind what you sense so we know what you have felt. Then ask for the guide to step right back out of your energy again. The exercise is now complete.

We would like to add here that if our energy gives you a

headache, makes you feel sick or gives you any other symptoms you don't like, it is unintentional. Simply ask us to take that discomfort away and draw back a bit from your energy field. Remember, we have to learn to work with you as a team, so make sure you tell us how you feel and we will adapt so you are comfortable.

This exercise is designed to strengthen your link with your guides and allow us to find the best way to work with you. If you do this exercise and don't feel us, TRUST we are there, connecting and hearing you. In the early days of development, if your energies are low, or you have great self-doubt, this can block us and weaken our connection with you. As you can see, you have to be aware of many things.

We see that as mediums develop and their mediumship muscle grows, they eventually realise one day they are not feeling their guides – don't panic if this happens to you, we haven't deserted you. It is simply that you have grown so used to our energies as you work with us, you no longer feel us as we draw in and out. Our medium friend has now experienced this, and when she does services or platform, she trusts that when she stands up to connect we are there, and of course we are.

We did mention about new guides coming to you at various points in life. When you are on the mediumship journey you will average about seven, with necessary changes made as you progress. When your energy is heightened you will sense a change. It might be a drop in energy or awareness of spirit around you. You can have physical symptoms such as palpitations, mild headaches and mood swings, which would only last a few days. If you have physical symptoms and feel unwell, ask your guides to help you as we give you healing in this transition period. BUT we must say if you suffer physical symptoms, don't put them all down to a new guide, as we would not leave you with long-term symptoms beyond the short period it takes us to adjust. If you get continued physical symptoms please visit a doctor to check all is OK with your health. If you sit in a development circle ask your teacher, they should know when you are having a change of guide as they will sense it from us and they will be able to advise you too.

Exercise 2 - Meditation to meet your guide

This is a visualisation meditation you can learn to do on your own or as a teacher to speak it in a group. It is written for a teacher to use.

Make sure all are sitting comfortably in a quiet room where you will not be disturbed. Play calming meditation music in the background.

Ask the participants to relax, uncross feet and arms and close their eyes.

Ask them to take a deep breath in, imagining they are breathing in healing and love; when they exhale, ask them to imagine they are breathing out any stress, anxiety and fear from their day. (Do this three times.)

Now imagine you are standing in a field on a beautiful summer's day. You can feel the healing warmth of the sun on your face. The sky is a beautiful blue with light fluffy clouds floating by.

As you look out in front of you, you can see a field full of long grass and wild flowers, a beautiful sight to behold. The flowers and grass are swaying gently in the summer breeze. In the distance you can see woodland and there is a path through the field to the wood.

Follow the path, running your hand gently through the flowers and grass as you go, feeling the warmth of the sun on your body. As you approach the woods you observe wonderful majestic trees and can feel the wisdom and healing energy they give out to Mother Earth.

Follow the moss path into the woods, the path feels soft under foot. You feel cooler now and notice the sunlight dancing through the tree canopy to the ground below. The birds are singing; take note of any wild life you observe as you walk along. In the distance there is the sound of running water.

As you carry on down the path the sound of water gets louder and you observe a gentle stream. The water sparkles as it jumps and flows over rocks and pebbles. The path starts to descend and the water is flowing quicker now. The path gently drops away and you can see an opening through the trees. As you reach it, a beautiful sight is front of you, a crystal clear pool with a waterfall flowing into it. The waterfall mesmerizes you as it sparkles in the sun and there are lots of tiny rainbows dancing in the water as it flows down into the pool. You feel so relaxed in this serene space of nature, knowing you feel safe and loved.

At the side of the pool there is a log and you sit down to take in the sun, pool and the beautiful setting. As you sit there we are going to invite one of your guides to join you on the log next to this beautiful pool. As they join you take their hand and just sit there with them and take in this beautiful space together. (Allow a minute of silence here with just music). *Now try and observe what they look like and ask their name.*

Your guide will now present you with a gift; this gift is for you and only you. A box is given to you; you open the lid and observe what the gift is. Ask your guide what meaning the gift has. (Give the student time to observe all this.)

Thank your guide for the gift and coming to meet you today. They will now leave you but will never be far away from you. Just spend a bit longer taking in this beautiful place, feeling the love and comfort you feel here.

It is time to return now. When you are ready to come back into the room, take a few deep breaths, wriggle you fingers and toes and open your eyes, take a couple of minutes and drink some water.

When everyone is ready, ask them in turn what they experienced, if they met their guide, got a name and a gift. Now remember, everyone will have a different experience, and not all minds cope with a visual meditation as they may not be very imaginative in life. But they should gain from the experience and we were definitely there with them on the visualisation journey they experienced.

Every time you sit with the energy of spirit we come and learn how to work better with you and adjust our own and your energies accordingly. So even if you come away feeling you did not visualise as much as the person next to you, just remember you are all on your own unique journey and gain from every experience with us.

You can adapt this meditation to meet your animal guides, just set the intent and add animal guide to the words. There are books on your earth that will tell you their meanings. So make sure you have one at hand if you do this in a circle, so the students can learn what their meaning are for them.

Spiritual writing

Another wonderful way to connect with your guides is spiritual writing. This is the next step on from exercise 2. Once you trust your connection and the words you receive in your head are from your guides, then the floodgates can open to our inspiration as you clear your mind of doubt. We have philosophers, poets and lots of wisdom among spirit, and we like nothing better than to channel our words to help humanity. We channel a lot of wisdom to humanity and have done for a long time, all to aid your ascension on Earth.

You can do spiritual writing in a development group or on your own.

It is best to find somewhere quiet to do your writing, again open in prayer, set the intent of what you wish to do and invite a guide to come forward to help you with inspirational words. If you are starting out you might get the odd word or two, but with practice, in no time you will have pages of wonderful inspiration and wisdom. Buy yourself a writing book to do this in to make it special to you.

Some of you might be urged to self-publish your writings; if you get this guidance please do so, as others will benefit from our words full of wisdom. We have added a few samples we have channeled through our medium friend while working on this book with her. Hopefully they will inspire you to write and trust the journey with us.

This is about our connection with you.

The Journey

As we step into your mind we see a million memories.
The stories of a time gone by in the layers of your cells.
A mishmash of a life jumbled by emotion and time.
We question my connection with your brain, waiting for trust.

We see your doubt of your feelings and emotions you feel.

We see your thoughts, is this real in my human mind?

As we progress on this journey together, we trigger your senses.

Your human mind tries to digest these new experiences.

We feel the balance of energy as we learn to trust each other.

The healing messages start to have meaning to others.

We witness your confidence grow and your energies clear.

We are now on a roll as we trust our connection to each other.

We witness you excel on this exciting journey of mediumship.

An experience that never stops growing and teaching you.

We will learn together my friend, always learning and trusting.

Now your messages bring the love and healing needed to humanity.

Our mission to help others is now sealed with ever lasting love.

We will always work in prayer of the divine love from above together.

This was for the animals that have no voice on Earth. But, my friends, they do – it's just that humanity blocks them and does not listen.

No Voice

I am a living being
Unique amongst many
I roam safe in my world
I am loved and nurtured

My kind understands me

As I grow my world changes
I feel fear and see death
My parents are no longer here
I wander in the wilderness
I am confused and alone

I am lost amongst many
But they are not my kind
My heart grows heavy
The truth hits me hard
I am alone across time

I am the last of my kind
I have a broken heart
I am growing weak
I take my last breath
My kind is now extinct

I am not part of your future
You will see me in a book
You will see me online
A memory of your time
All I ask is WHY?

A small reminder your children are your future, let them reach their full potential in their lives.

I am the future

I am a star child full of love
I am your future so treat me well
Let me be I, to reach my potential
Nurture me with love and honesty
I have great purpose on Mother Earth
My power lies within reaching the stars
I am a unique being the only one of me
Treasure the child I wish to be.

.

Section 4

The journey of the medium

When you take the spiritual path it will affect you and the world around you, especially in friendships and relationships. You do not have to be a medium or healer to be a spiritual person. Being a spiritual person is someone whose highest priority is to be loving to yourself and others. Someone who cares about people, animals and your Mother Earth and they know that we are all One, and consciously attempts to honour this Oneness. And most of all they are kind, always seeking peace and the good for the greater good of humanity. The mediums and healers of your world lead the way on the spiritual way of being, setting the example for others to follow.

Anyone who follows the spiritual path will naturally shed what does not serve them and eventually attract their true soul tribe. This is the human's from your soul group in the spirit realm here to connect with you on a higher level as you raise your energies. Remember the three-dimensional energy grid, each human has an individual energy that functions in this grid. When we look at you we see an energy light, those that have not found the spiritual love path, their light is a bit dull in the three-dimensional energy grid. As you progress on the spiritual path, it can be, anyone, healer or a medium your light starts to shine brighter. This is because you become a tuned to the higher unconditional love energy of the fifth dimension to allow you to strengthen your connection with us. To other humans that have not attuned to this way of being they can have difficulty dealing being near to your newfound bright energy burst. They know something is different but cannot comprehend what it is. Some might be become more negative with jealousy or just find it difficult to be a round you because of your new bright light. You also will find it difficult to be around negative people yourself.

We have been on this journey with our medium friend and she now knows not to fear this when it happens to her, as it still does. She now accepts this as part of her spiritual process sending love and light to those who step back from her journey. As we have discovered, you shed the negative energy and draw in the positive energy and the more love and light people nearer to you. Also note, not all people go out of your life for good; they stay there as part of your everyday existence, but they are more in the background as you learn to protect yourself from the negative energy they direct at you.

You will have a lot of people drift in and out of your life while on this spiritual journey, all for various reasons, all of them traveling their own journey and truth. From our experience with our medium friend we have placed this is to three groups to help you understand.

Group one: *The Distant Group* – This group is mainly family and friends who have pulled away and distanced themselves from you for various reasons that you might never know while on the earth plane. Some of these people might get involved in your spiritual journey; go to spiritual events and workshops you attend, as they want to part of what's changing your life for the better. But for some reason on their path they become resentful and jealous as your light shines brighter. Remember this was their truth not yours, the lesson for you is not to hold malice against them, but send them love and light and hope they find happiness and learn to love themselves better. Some people are unhappy and they lash out at others, sometimes even from their subconscious. It is best not to seek answers as to why, but to accept this is for the greater good in your life. Worrying about why what could have been uses up your good energies.

Group two: *The Contemplators Group* – This group is made up of family and friends who accept you and the changes they see in you even if they do not understand it yet. They might come to the odd event, workshop, and medium reading and healing with you. Their experiences are making them question their existence and path in life. They are experiencing things they do not understand, new feelings, and feeling and seeing spirit around them. They are excited by their new journey but also a bit doubtful and working to build their trust in what they are experiencing. They ask questions about spirit and quietly contemplate your answers; they will not be 100% believers yet, but you have let the spirit realm into their thoughts, which could be a start of their own spiritual journey.

Group three: *The Accepters Group* – these are family and friends who are intrigued and fully accept and understand you as you are. These are the people in your life who have supported your journey, and been excited themselves by their own experiences, gained from workshops, events and messages. Some of them are taking their first steps with spirit, finding spiritualism, or perhaps working with spirit on the healing path. They might start taking their first steps on their Reiki journey. They might write their spirit journey one day, as our medium friend – who knows? But the awesome thing is you will have been a small part of their journey. You are all connected and your paths intertwine, nudging each other along your paths, with your spirit guides helping behind the scenes.

We do witness in the early days of your mediumship journey, you will want to steam ahead in the new found excitement and do everything you can for development. We do love to see your excitement my friend but our advice would be to slow down your pace, trust and accept that it will flow as needed when it should. Your spiritual journey will start at different points in your lives. Our medium friend was in her forties. She did not understand this and why it was not in her teens or twenties, as she felt there was so much she could have done to help people. Well, in her case it was the life experiences, good or bad, that were needed to help heal others and quite often related to her clients we send her. Remember we show you your own past memories and experiences, to give evidence in readings, to help connect with people for

51

healing messages and guidance from the spirit realm.

Light workers and Earth angels

We hope you have heard of Earth angels and light workers. You can be sure to have encountered them in your life so far and there will be many more in the years ahead.

Light workers and Earth angels are here to bring light, love and healing to Mother Earth. The light workers living among you will be drawn to the world of healing, for example, nurses, doctors, vets, conservationist, holistic healers and mediums. Both will be here for the highest good of various people, animals and plants that they were caring for.

The characteristics of both will appear wise beyond their years and carry deep-set knowledge and understanding of energy, different dimensions and higher realms.

Light workers are here to teach to others about the light within and guide them on a healing journey. Also which is key to your ascension to remind you of your intuition. Intuition is from your spirit within (soul), which is a gift from spirit. Once humanity can connect to this and harness it in their everyday life, it enhances their connection with the universe and us. They will be selfless people here to help Mother Earth in whatever their chosen mission is. Their light shines very bright for others to follow, always setting the example of what all humanity could be and expire to.

Our medium friend sees light workers as people that heal, work in the light way of being helping others on a lighter path, not just spiritual work. She is correct, as light workers are those among you that make a difference to others life's to make it better than it was before. Through their work others will see a better way of being, leading them to a better-ascended way of living. This often encourages others to take a job change to be a holistic healer or, say, a medium.

Earth Angels are here to give key direction to you at important life path decisions. They might be in your life for a few seconds, minutes, days or months, but not a lifetime. They will make you feel connected and loved. They might give you information you need for future decisions. They could be the voice in your head to slow down when driving or they could be the man that pulls you off the road before you are hit by a bus and he is never seen again. They are not always seen or sometimes heard, feeling a physical contact you cannot understand. We do not try to intervene too much on the life path, but remember the 99.9% where there is that small chance something that we could not foresee will knock you off a life path mission. We will plan interaction with Earth angels at key points in your life. Hopefully you will connect with these messages to guide you on a future decision.

Positive way of being

Key for your spiritual path is to live in the positive energy vibration. A lot of you on Earth are starting to understand the negative and positive energies. We see a lot of you still doubt and question these theories and that it can help humanity move forward. The only thing that stops this negative/positive theory working is you with the fears, anxieties and illusions you create in your minds about the world you live in. This holds you back on your life's path keeping you in the negative three dimensional energy streams.

To move forward my friends you need to resolve these issues within your human essence to allow the energy to flow freely around your body. This will allow the positive energy to become strong in the love and light and the negative energies to fade.

You do all create a path before you come to a physical existence in the universe, yours at this time is to be on Earth. We are aware of events that might affect your life's path and knock you of course a bit, but as we have said we cannot be a hundred per cent on this. There will be things that come on to your pathway we had not anticipated, but we deal with this as it happens from the spirit realm with your spirit within and guides that help to get you back on track.

The ones that doubt this negative and positive energy theory, and the creation of a reality through affirmations, manifestations, thoughts and words to help humanity move forward, believe that some humans are so broken within through traumas within their physical human life that they cannot be helped by this theory.

We do see when humans hurt each other and how it affects the human essence and it takes a great deal of healing. While you are in the 3D dimension sometimes healing is needed from the medical professions on your earth as well as the spiritual realm encouraging the positive way of being. As you ascend in to your 4D dimension the healing will use your human mind and the spirit within to heal you without your medical nurses and doctors. This is because as you move into the 4D energy, the harm humans cause each other through abuse and the crimes against humanity will decrease and there will not be so many broken humans in your world crying out with pain and fear what their life's can bring to them. Your minds will start to reset them self's bringing clarity and greater understanding to the human race.

As you ascend in to the 5D dimension and have faith my friends, as humanity will heal themselves, there will be no sickness of the body or mind and no medicines will be needed. The world will be a different place to what you know it today and humanity will heal themselves. There will no longer be fear, anxiety and hate amongst mankind to cause harm to other humans and animals.

So you can see the picture we are trying to show you with

our words, it's just to have faith and trust in what we are saying about creating your own life into positive way of being.

NOW, have a thought. Why should you not have life full of abundance, health, wealth, a nice house and nice cars? You can still be a beautiful person within, being kind and helping others in your world. You can bring in an abundance of love and wealth through this positive energy with thoughts, words and affirmations we have been talking about.

This positive pure energy from the love and light of the spirit realm and universe will be drawn to those of you that have a positive attitude with pure heart and good intentions. Those of you that chose to manifest and pretend to be in the love and light will draw more negative energies in and will struggle to achieve your goals. This is because the universe and spirit realm know the true intent that lies with-in you, not the outside façade you are pretending to be. This is what the universe picks up on and that is what you will receive back to your energies. Those that draw in the negative energies will have their problems, ill health, regret and strife in life and they will not heal their fears and concerns and health.

To make this easy for you we split it into the Positive and Negative energies. The words we use and the way we say them is key to this change of bringing positive energy. So take the first step my friend and change your thought pattern today. Which are you?

Positive or **Negative**.

Negative energy	Positive energy
Hate	Love
Miserable	Happy
Dark	Light
Obstacle	Experience
Greif	Acceptance
Cry	Smile
Cruel	Kind
Dictatorship	Freedom
Rough	Smooth
Lost	Found
Dark	Light
Negative	Positive
Mistake	Lesson
Die	Live
Punish	Forgive
Frown	Smile
Sick	Well
Distance	Near
Selfish	Share
Shut	Open
Nothing	Plenty

Negative energy	Positive energy
Silence	Speak
Degrade	Uplift
Jail	Sanctuary
Deflate	Inspire
Hit	Hug
Sly	Honest
Deceit	Transparency
Disconnect	Connect
Broken	Whole
Mist	Clear
Nothing	Universe
Addiction	Clean
Fake	Real
Lie	Truth
Take	Give
Despair	Elevated
Distraught	Euphoric
Depressed	Happy
Ugly	Beautiful
Unperceptive	Insight

You can see from this list of words what we mean; you change your way of thinking and actions to others by changing your thought patterns and words. Practice this in your everyday lives and you will see such a difference.

Heal yourselves

We see on your earth a world of too much sickness, pain and too much fear my friends. The fears are survival based for example - Where is the next meal coming from? How can we afford these bills? Who's going to help us? Why is this happening to us? You can see the negativity in this fear by these words alone.

We know that humanity can heal themselves through positive thoughts and energy, because you see in simple terms when you become ill its through the stress of your lives. In the western world it's more to do with your pace of life that causes anxiety and stress. In other areas of the world it can be nature, man-made situations in war torn countries, religious differences and stress that these situations cause. All of this is surrounded by the negative energy and your body adsorbs this negative energy, which then manifests in the body. You can imagine where there is poor diet and inhumane treatment the poor humans caught up in this struggle to find any positive energies. This is where the rest of humanity can come in and help each other and bring the positive energies to these people that need it.

When humans become sick, including the terminal illnesses amongst you, humans worry and fear and think why me? We see this as natural way for you after thousands of years of this way thinking, BUT it is time to reboot your brains, and get out of this negative way of thinking. When you are sick you draw more negative energies into your body and the sickness within you will collect it and feed of it making the symptoms worse. Have you noticed when you are stressed or have high anxiety any ailment you suffer with increases, this is because the negative energy targets the weak areas of your bodies and mind. You need to build the positive energy to flow round these weaker areas to protect them and let them heal.

Now for those of you that have lost loved ones to sickness on your Earth it is hard for you to understand this as you have seen the pain they have suffered and the pain that reflects around the surviving loved ones and friends. BUT do TRUST my friends that you can heal yourselves and humanity. If you could all from the moment you are born, be taught to think in the positive vein of love and kindness, this would bring your Mother Earth back to a balanced energy again and humanity will not suffer the illnesses', the anguish and the fear it suffers now.

There are healers amongst you around your world that are starting to understand this and spread the word to others. Some of these healers we mention have healed them selves even from your diseases and mental illnesses from this positive way of thinking and trusting in the divine for help with this.

We know you understand by now the 3D energy that you

exist in at the moment and as more and more of you start to think in the positive energy, changing your thought pattern and your words you will ascend in to the 4D energy. It is as simple as saying when you wake up every day, 'I am well', and I am balanced'. If a doctor tells you have something wrong, or you develop a viral illness, visualize yourself without it and visualize yourself well, and ask for healing from your angels and guides of pure love and light energy. Remember the negative energy, this is attracted to you when you are ill as your mind set goes in to negative way of thinking and your mind and energy field can be clouded if you have pain with your illness or health condition.

You also need to look at why did I get this condition or illness, was it through unhealthy eating and no exercise, or is it from the stress that's in my life? You need to sort out in your own life's the stress, the fears and anxieties that lie within you from the traumas that have been on your human path while on earth.

We know the understanding of the positive and negative energies will help you with your mediumship path. There will be times you doubt yourself or others cast a shadow over your journey. Just pick up this handbook to remind yourself of how you can change for the better, to be a good channel and advocate for spirit.

Section 5

Self-awareness, meditation and mindfulness

It is key on this journey of discovery to be a medium that you are very self-aware. What we mean by this is you know your own body, and energy and you keep your energy balanced and grounded. We also feel it is key to healing and lifting your energy vibration that you have self-awareness of their own body and spirit within. As you develop this awareness of self, this will help build your connections with us and one thing that will help with this is to bring meditation and mindfulness into your lives. Meditation when mastered is away of saying your mind, body and soul are free to go anywhere, taking you deeply as you can to the spirit realm. When you master meditation, your human mind is like a beautiful painting that can take you on a journey to eliminate distractions of past and future worries. Then this opens the door to inner peace and health. You learn to carry on this new awareness and clarity into everyday life with mindfulness.

In the spirit realm, we have great knowledge of meditation and mindfulness and being aware of the moment, we don't have time, as you know it in your limited third dimension energy. We live in the fifth dimension energy where we do not follow a time-constrained existence; this helps to give us great awareness and clarity of everything around us. Our thought stream is telepathic by nature, and we have great control over our mind links and when we connect to others. We are aware of what's gone before also considering the future, but we don't let these thoughts or words affect our energy or the decisions we take in the now moment.

We have been encouraging meditation and mindfulness practice among humans for centuries – look at some of your Eastern countries for the history of this. In your western world it is becoming a welcome trend at the moment, as the light builds and more and more light workers are teaching this and making others aware. This should be part of all mediumship development and is something you can work on yourself as well in a development circle.

Meditation

Meditation is key to any medium's development, as it helps calm the mind opening up clear channels to hear or see us.

The Earth word meditation, is derived from two Latin words: meditari(to think, to dwell upon, to exercise the mind) and mederi (to heal). Its Sanskrit derivation 'medha' means wisdom, which we feel sums up the word meditation well in your language.

With the hectic pace and demands of your modern Earth life's, many people feel stressed and over-worked. It often feels like there is just not enough time in the day to get everything done. Your stress and tiredness make you unhappy, impatient and frustrated and it can even affect your health. You are often so busy you feel there is no time to stop and meditate! But meditation actually gives you more time by making your mind calmer and more focused. You will learn to put first what is important in life, and as you distress every day tasks will be come easier.

Meditation can also help you to understand our own mind. You learn how to transform your mind from negative thoughts to positive thoughts, from disturbed to peaceful, from unhappy to happy.

In meditation, you are shifting your awareness from the usual focus, of past and future to the now moment creating calmness in the mind. In daily activity, the mind is engaged in observing, discriminating, deciding, analyzing and accomplishing. Meditation gives you the opportunity to shift gears, let go of this focus and experience a more peaceful, silent state of being.

Different types of meditation

The aim of any meditation is to create a relaxed state of body and mind; the mind is awake but calm. Have you heard of the earth scientific terms of alpha and beta brain levels? Beta is when you are fully awake, making decisions, focusing on past, present and future and using up energy. In the physical beta state the blood is pumping hard to all vital organs using high energy.

Alpha is the relaxed brain state but you are not a sleep. Imagine as you get in to bed and you have washed your sheets and they smell fresh and clean. You snuggle down and relax, but awake, that's the calm feeling you need to reach. In alpha state the blood flow as the body relaxes goes more to the outer shell than the inner body.

We want to achieve this meditative state of being in the moment, relaxed and de-stressed. When stressed you produce a hormone that you can get addicted to, becomes a cycle of a way of being and your body if it has any physical weaknesses will react to stress through these manifesting themselves more ten fold. Good mental state, calmness and focus all helps the physical well being as well as the mind.

Remember meditation does not have to be complex. Key to successful mediation is finding which one that suits you. There are a few different ways you can meditate listed below:

o With music – guided with a voice and music

o Mantra meditation

o On the spot meditation – Mindfulness

o Sitting in the silence building your inner power

Meditation guided with voice and music

We find observing the human mind that a lot of you when starting mediation will find listening to a guided meditation works best for you to start with. Start of with one that is for relaxation and help you to distress. Then when you are feeling more confident with this form of mediation, try more spiritual mediations for example we mean, linking you with your guides and helping your spiritual connection for mediumship. We recommend you email our medium friend and she will advice the ones that have helped her on her journey with us, which is at the end of the book.

As with all meditation samples here they work by distracting you from your daily thoughts and help you to calm your mind. It is key to find meditations that you are comfortable with. Observing our medium friend teach meditation, we soon learnt how each individual human minds and energy is affected by different tone pitches in music and spoken voice. This is because you all have individual energy frequencies and the vibration of sound affects you differently as individuals. So finding the right type of tone from music or the spoken voice and the intention of the meditation is vital to success on the meditation journey.

Mantra meditation

In mantra meditations, you repeat a particular sound or short phrase again and again. This can be done out loud (chanting) or in your mind. It is key you pick a mantra that has spiritual meaning on your path at this time and then later changes in intervals as you grow. Repeating words with positive vibration and positive uplifting intention helps to recondition you mind and self-belief of who you are and what you can achieve. This leads to clarity in your thinking, and will help you be on a higher vibration and this helps us work with you telepathically, mind-to-mind with your mediumship.

Using a mantra affirmation while you're meditating helps suppress the thoughts and distractions that arise and gives you a tool to use when you're not meditating. Repeating a meditation mantra during times of stress, for many people, brings about some relaxation and helps them to better deal with whatever the crisis of the moment is. Depending on your belief system, the mantras may also do things like get you in touch with the true nature of the universe, help you spiritually and activate energy centres in the body.

Remember your thoughts are energy and when you do this type of meditation you need to believe what you are repeating and keep in the positive energy mind frame. So as you let doubt come in to it, it affects the energy and how the manta will work. You can ask your guides, spiritual teacher or meditation teacher to help guide you to the write manta for that point in your spiritual journey.

When you could pick your mantra – it could be a

simple word like "relax," "serene" "love" or "peace," or something more spiritual like "ohm" or "so-hum" (ancient Sanskrit words meaning "nothingness" and "I am that").

Assume a comfortable but alert upright position, and spend 30 seconds just sitting with your eyes closed before starting your mantra breathing steadily. As effortlessly and silently as possible, begin repeating your mantra to yourself (not aloud), over and over. A good method is to get into a smooth breathing pattern, with the words being said in your head on the outward breath. If your mind wanders, just observe the thought, let it pass by and go back to repeating the mantra. The more you practice, the easier this will become for you. There's no need to try to change or stop your thoughts in anyway – just keep whispering the word(s) silently to yourself. The repetition of a mantra quiets the breath and as a result the mind, according to bringing you into the field of "pure consciousness." From a beginner's perspective, using a mantra can help focus and sharpen a mind prone to wandering during meditation. As our medium friend does, if you are on your own while doing this ask us to stop you after 15 minutes. Then just bring yourself back into your space and sit for a bit reflecting on how you feel.

As we said you can do one-word mantras or try something longer. A few suggestions for Present Tense Affirmations you:

My mind is clear and focused

My body is relaxed and calm

I am at peace within myself

I am focused on the present moment

A few suggestions for Future Tense Affirmations you:

My mind is becoming quiet and relaxed

I will release all stress and tension

I am finding it easier to detach from my thoughts

I will let go of all worries

A few suggestions for Natural Affirmations you:

My mind is naturally calm and tranquil

I have a peaceful mind

Mental serenity is mine

I can let go of my thoughts at will

The 'I am' moments

We would also suggest what we call the **'I am'** affirmations, to become aware of self and raise your energies this way.

The **'I am'** moment is key to you lifting your energies; remember this all starts with you. We suggest you do an 'I am' meditation mantra for five minutes each day when you awake, repeating the chosen affirmation to reinforce the positive energy vein in your lives. We have listed a few below for you to try:

I am Love and joy

I am happy

I am willing to let go

I am the best I can be

I am beautiful

I am loved

I am strong and powerful

I am calm

I am at peace

I am loved

On the spot meditations – Mindfulness

We know this is a positive way forward for humanity to help you connect more with yourself, the world around you and us. Learning and understanding mindfulness will also aid you in meditation, which helps to de-stress you, clearing and raising your energies to aid ascension in the energy levels.

The benefits of mindfulness help in these ways:

- o It cultivates more awareness and stabilises the mind

- o You become clear-seeing (have clarity) in everything around you and within yourself

- o It changes your perspective on your world and your thought patterns

- o It brings wisdom, as you see your world differently

o It helps de-stress you by casting worrying thoughts to the side and giving your busy mind a rest.

Your minds are amazing things, with great power that could unfold great things for you as a individual. At the moment your minds are restricted by dwelling on you're past memories and emotions, which then influence how you look at your future. Your mind is judgmental and creates its own miss-perceptions of situations and the world around you.

Your mind connects to your senses – sight, hearing, touch, smell and taste. We see you see without seeing, hear without hearing, touch without touching, smell without smelling and taste without truly tasting. You also have another sense, **Knowing**, which is like a sixth sense and is in your mind field and your energy field. What do we mean? Knowing is something that you use without realising it, but it is a weak sense at the moment in most of you. When tapped into and strengthened, this ability will bring you knowledge from the universe, clarity to your thinking, wisdom and greater understanding. And very importantly it helps with your development as medium and strengthens your connection to us. This is because when your mind is less busy we can connect telepathically to you better. Also this will help a medium learn to have a less busy mind when giving messages and focus on the clear spirit thoughts and images coming in.

You rush along in your world, thinking you are aware of the world around you, but you are not. The simplest way for us to describe this in words is to give an example: You are given ten red pencils laid out next to each other in a row; most people will think they are all the same and not take a second look at them; as long as they function and serve the purpose that is all that matters. BUT each pencil is unique! If you stopped and looked at each individual pencil, you would be able to describe each one and the uniqueness that makes them different from each other. As you did this you would be more aware of that moment in time, as if you have slowed down time to stop and become aware of these 10 red pencils. You can feel them, look at them all over, smell them, listen to them and even taste them. When you are this aware you are being **mindful, and this is what mindfulness means.**

We do laugh though – we say be more aware, but if you followed this example of the red pencils to everything in your day, you would not get much done! BUT do you see what we are saying?

To help you on the path of mindfulness we are going to give you a couple of simple exercises to get you started. But we recommend you find a good meditation teacher to guide you.

Breathing exercise

Shut your eyes.

Now concentrate your attention on your breath, your normal everyday breathing pattern. The breath will be centre stage of your awareness, just let your body breathe for itself as we do every day.

Take your awareness to the gentle flowing of the IN and OUT breath, notice how it feels travelling up and down your airways to your lungs. How does it feel in your nostrils, and then as your breath flows to your lungs?

Feel the breath leaving the body and re-entering. Where do you feel the sensations? In the nostrils, mouth, stomach? Relax and just ride the waves of your breathing moment by moment, with each breath. Remind yourself of the attention you need to give this, concentrating on the breathing.

Can you smell the breath, is there any taste and are there sensations in your mouth?

Imagine the breath blowing out. Does it have colour, or is there any moisture?

If any past and present thoughts intrude, just gently and lovingly let the thoughts pass by, re-establishing focus on the breath. Refocus as earlier on the nostrils, lungs and stomach.

Now expand your awareness to your whole body. How does the breath feel? Your skin breathes – can you feel this and take note of any sensations you pick up on?

Now take yourself back to focusing on the nostrils, the breath coming in and out of the body. Just rest on these feelings, being in the moment, and when you feel ready, go back to normal activities.

This is a simple everyday exercise for you to use, to help bring clarity and rest to your busy mind. The more you practice this the better it will be, and you will be able to do it for longer periods when your third dimension busy energy life allows.

Glass of water exercise

Sit in a chair near a table and place by you a glass of water.

When you are ready, pick up the glass of water and hold it in both hands. Hold the glass in front of your face so you can clearly see it with your eyes. Examine the glass and see what you observe. Is it smooth, is it rough, is it dull, is it chunky, is the glass thin or thick, is there any scratches on it, and are there colours or reflections?

Now notice the temperature of the glass.

Now move the glass carefully around to one of your ears and gently rotate it in your hand. Do you notice any sound?

Now take the glass and lift it to your mouth, but before you swallow any water, smell the glass and notice any odors. Also take notice of how your mouth feels inside — is it dry, is there any saliva?

Now swallow some of the water. How does the water feel? Is it smooth, is it cold, is it warm, what does it taste like and does it cause sensations in your mouth?

Take another sip and imagine following the water from the mouth to your stomach, seeing it on its journey inside you. Notice any sensations.

When you feel ready, set the glass back on the table and reflect on your experience.

This second simple exercise again really takes your awareness to the uniqueness of the glass of water, something you all take for granted every day.

After reading this section we now feel you are beginning to understand where we are coming from on the ideas of mindfulness and raising your awareness. Practice regularly, my friends, and see where it takes you. If you struggle with this find a meditation teacher to help you and seek guidance from your circle you attend.

Self-discovery is key to the mediumship journey.

Section 6

Different ways you can start developing to work with the spirit realm

Every human has the capability to be a medium and there have been many humans who have used this gift over your Earth centuries. Many of those that had found their power and built on it were destroyed by those that were fearful of this unseen source. It's only been in the last 20 years that we have witnessed greater acceptance of mediums in your world. This is in the parts of your world where freethinking is allowed and mediums have the confidence not to hide what they do any more with the fear of reprisals. Also we have noticed through time that a lot of these mediums and healers use items like crystals, cards, crystal balls and for example Ouija boards for connecting to the spirit realm. We are happy to work with you on this basis, because the human part of you needs this safety net, this link that you believe helps connects you to us. In the three-dimensional world you live in at the moment, the fear of failure and lack of trust is one of the reasons why you still use these objects. You know inside to trust that we are there, but you feel you need some sort of solid connection to us because you don't all see clearly our spirit realm but feel our energies. You still hold an inner fear of what you cannot see and understand the energies around you.

We have also realised that the clients who come to you looking for answers about their future, or want to hear from a loved one or for some healing, will feel more at ease if they see you using objects. These can be essences, crystals, cards, pendulums or whatever it is you have been drawn to use. Because some clients don't understand about spirit, they see the connection of the items you are using, or believe that the item is bringing forth the source that is making them feel better.

But what we would like to say to you is that you can connect to spirit with trust, with no fear and with the right intent of healing and love for all your clients. We always will work with you, so that the person in front of you will receive exactly what they need without you needing any items to help. Your trust will help you sense when we tell you that enough is enough, and it's time to stop the reading or healing session. Through trust, message givers such as mediums will receive the information and guidance needed for a client.

Every medium and healer works in a different way with different objects, and what is important is every message you give, opens up a light in the heart of the person receiving your help, bringing them a step nearer to spirit and healing. Because we are trying to help you ascend and become better humans, we need to make you aware of this.

We are intrigued by the history behind mankind's objects you use for mediumship healing and protection, you will be surprised at how long they have been in place. For your interest, we have included some here for you.

Candles - They have been a symbol for humanity for centuries, used in religions, celebrations in life, and simply for giving light in a home. Imagine the magic of that first flame, and the discovery of wax and a wick. Picture the magic of this event in your time line, developing these things that then led to these life-changing events. Candles have been used for light and to illuminate humanity's celebrations for more than 5,000 years. The Egyptians were using wicked candles in 3,000 B.C; the ancient Romans were developing the wicked candle before that time, by dipping rolled papyrus repeatedly in melted tallow or beeswax. The resulting candles were used to light their homes, to aid travelers at night, and in religious ceremonies. The use of candles soon spread to more advanced cultures, with candle making techniques evolving over time.

Think: when you discover spirit, your vibration/energy is lifted, and this sends out a beacon of light into the darkness of space, like a candle. Humans believe candles can help to invite in spirit, and they are also a symbol of memory at a loved one's parting. When a candle is lit with this intent, it lets the spirit realm know you're thinking of them. They also set a lovely ambiance in your working space for the clients.

Crystal ball - Crystal gazing was commonly practiced by your earth people the Pawnee, the Iroquois, the Incas, the

Egyptians, the Persians, the Chinese, and the people of Yucatan. These first adopters of crystal gazing would stare deeply into the stone, falling into a meditative trance that would allow the subconscious to open up to give messages, healing and guidance.

The act of gazing into a reflective or translucent surface to glean prophetic insight came to be known as scrying, and the practice was used on literally anything, including blood, water and mirrors, although crystal balls are the most common mechanism for this type of connecting with the unseen energy of the divine. The focus they used when gazing took them in to a trance state, calming their minds and linking them to spirit and other ascension beings.

The early crystal gazers, or specularii, preferred a sea-green mineral called Beryl, which was polished into spheres to enhance its reflective properties, the start of the crystal ball. The crystal ball has appeared across the world in various shapes and form, but the one to which you mostly relate in the western world is the image of a woman, usually thought to be a "gypsy," traveling in their caravans with their crystal ball. They would deliver messages to whoever would listen, for the price of a coin crossing the palm.

Crystals - We would like to point out that crystals have a power of their own and you are right to assume they have an individual power, of which the spirit realm has made humanity aware. Crystals also have a way of recording and holding information and energy, so that's why it is important they are cleansed regularly if you use them on your clients as a form of healing connection. We do use them to help channel into a human body if available; but we do not need them, as we divert the healing energy ourselves to where it needs to go in the human body.

Pendulum – The pendulum has been used by your healers and mediums for a long time through your history. Historically, it has also been used for dowsing and has been known for its ability to locate water, gold, oil and other minerals, and is still used to this day in parts of your world. But we would mainly like to talk about the use of the crystal pendulums used by healers and mediums today.

They are often used to pick up energy areas within the human body that need healing, by connecting with a break in good energy flow. The healer connects with their healers in spirit, who work with them and guide them to where their hands should be placed. You can also trust and use your hands; we will give you sensations to pick this up if you do not wish to use the pendulum. But trust, and we will guide your hands to where we need them to go.

Some use the pendulum to connect to the spirit realm as confirmation in your life's looking for yes and no answers. We put a word of caution round this, if you are not protected and using it with out good intent, spirit that are still earth bound or other unseen forces you do not yet understand will be drawn to you, they will play with it and can give false information, so be careful my friends.

Incense - When ancient humans discovered fire they soon realised that when they burnt wood and leaves, most materials give off a unique and sometimes powerful aroma. The difference between the smell of a handful of leaves and that of a pine tree branch is greatly emphasized when each is burnt.

There is historic evidence in most of your earth cultures that people used incense burning for sacred, cleansing and healing purposes. From ancient times, people recognized that aromas produced by burning materials could heighten the senses, both sight and smell. When early man gathered around their fires, the smell of aromatic woods, herbs and leaves carried by heavenwards spirals of smoke was a rare sensory pleasure. A lot of them developed this as a way of worshipping their gods.

They discovered that the benefits of burning incense included the purification of an area, to change a mood to facilitate meditation or religious practices, and to cleanse living spaces after death or illness. Also used today as a practice of protection called smudging, where healers and mediums cleanse a space of negative energy. Again, my friends, this can be done with prayer; it is the intent of healing, love and light that clears these negative energies, the combination of both is very powerful.

Cards – A lot of psychics and mediums use cards for

giving messages. They become familiar with a pack they are drawn to, using the beautiful images and symbols on them as triggers for messages and their meanings. We work with you to use the cards, the symbols and images for giving the basis of a message which helps open your mind to us, so we can then feed in what we have to say to you. We see two sides to you using cards. First of all a lot of mediums start of using cards to help aid their readings and eventuality discard them as their power of connection, confidence and trust grows. But we are wise enough to realise that people whom are drawn to these readings like to see the cards as the giver of the messages. Also the reading given can be a trigger point on their spiritual path, as with all the objects we have mentioned.

Ouija boards – Ouija boards have been around for almost two of your centuries; they were very popular at one time, used by mediums in the western world as a way of demonstrating a physical way of communicating with the spirit realm. We give you a word of caution about this way of communicating: if it is not done in prayer and protection, you open the power of your thought to all out there in the energies of earth and beyond. This includes energies not of the spirit realm, from other dimensions, and the layers of unseen forces that surround Mother Earth. This is a similar warning we gave with the pendulum; with this method, you could get false messages and physical activity can happen that you cannot control, and do not have the experience to handle. When you need to communicate with the spirit realm and want to use a Ouija board, my friends, use a experienced medium to guide you.

We hope you enjoyed the samples given and the history behind them. If you are drawn to work with one of the samples given then please try it. Just be aware of the caution guidance given with some of them.

Teaching exercises

We thought it would be useful to add to this book some basic level teaching exercises for new spiritual teachers to use in their circles to aid development and give you some advice. It will also help you the developing medium to understand the type of exercises you would do in a circle or workshop.

To the teacher: we feel students should be allowed to develop as a medium with their own personality shining through. The uniqueness of the human essence and spirit within mix makes a very interesting person. Also, their guides will be matched to their personalities, influencing their personalities too when they work. A client will warm to the natural genuine medium, giving evidence in humour, laughter and honest approach. Yes, you need structure to the teaching, but letting the student find their own way on their unique path is key. We will bring students to you that suit your personality and style of teaching. Now as a teacher you will become fond of your students, but don't let your ego affect your teaching, as if there is only your way to teach. You must let your students go out and do different things and find their own path. Let them go out in the world to develop their own mediumship personality, show their uniqueness and let their own charm shine through in their messages. Their experiences of life will be key, as we bring forth the people the medium can give messages to who have had similar experiences in life and understand what they have gone through. As the teacher, keep your doors open to your students as their path might lead them back to you.

To the student: remember you can have more than one teacher, if you feel guided when more experienced to sit in more than one circle and attend various workshops, then please do, as to find your true mediumship style you need more than one teacher to achieve this. Don't be a robotic medium. By this, we mean finding the same sort of evidence for each reading such as, sex, height, how they died, job and dates. Let us use your personality and energy to bring forth the spirit's personality and simple, good pieces of evidence that suit the individual spirit. For example, one night while waiting to go on platform, our medium friend saw in her mind's eye a young lad in a wheelchair. Nothing unusual, perhaps, but the spirit boy was doing wheelies and spinning it around on one wheel for over half an hour. As our medium friend stood up she trusted to give this information out to the audience. She knew he was like this in life before he got ill and wanted to show what he was like again in spirit – full of energy. His mother was in the audience and she said that's my son. Now there was no need for further evidence, but his grandfather did come through too, with some family guidance. The son's message was simple: 'Look at me, I am healed now.'

These are all teaching exercises that we have seen work well with our medium friend through her teachings. We have covered grounding, meditation and mindfulness in Section 4 already. These next exercises are helping you build your links with your guides, the psychic energy and the mediumship mind-to-mind connection.

1. Strengthen the connection with your guides

This is a group teaching exercise as we ask the student to speak their guides' thoughts out loud. It is also a good confidence booster for speaking when they eventually do services or platform. If you are a mediumship development teacher this is a good exercise for your circle or workshops.

First of all select a group of words, at least 20, for example love, child, wisdom, beauty, Earth, basically inspiring words, which are individually placed on small cards. Select one for the person who will be doing the exercise, and we will guide you to a suitable word for them. Ask them to stand and say the word out loud, and what the word means to them as they are now in their daily life's, not connected to their guides. No more than a minute's explanation is needed here of what it means to them. Then ask them to ask a guide to step forward into their energy field as close as they can, to give them their guide's take on the word. The chosen guide will influence their mind with their thoughts and words. If they are new to this exercise let them do it with their eyes closed. They might receive one word, a sentence, verses or a vision. When they have finished ask them to sit down and explain what they experienced, for example feeling the guide's energy, what they saw or heard. Ask others what they observed; they should notice a difference in the chosen person's energy as the guide came forward. There could also be a change in the language they used when they spoke.

Now this exercise is a wonderful way to build trust with your spirit guides. It is connecting with the light trance energy and the student trusting what enters their mind and giving these thoughts in words over to the room.

If you are with more advanced students they can do this exercise with their eyes open as if they are addressing a congregation of people. It's a good confidence building exercise for developing mediums when they give spiritual guidance at services with their guides influence.

2. Learning to read cards

Make sure you have a varied selection of packs of cards for your students to choose from. (Our medium friend has a mixed range of angel, fairy and nature cards.)

Place the students in pairs and ask them to pick a pack of

cards they are drawn to.

When seated opposite each other, ask them to discard the booklet and box, as these are not needed.

Ask them to choose who is to go first and ask the lead reader to clear the deck of any energy from previous readings. This can be done with intent of prayer.

It is the student medium's choice whether they pick the cards or let their client shuffle the pack and pick them. Whichever way, they will be guided to the right cards needed for that reading.

This is a three-card reading, with the first card for the past, the middle card for the present, and the last card for future guidance. The cards are placed face down left to right.

The reader starts with the past card, working through to the present, and finishing with the future card.

The cards are used to inspire the visual senses and the words of the mind. One medium might look at the pictures only, another at the words on the card or they may connect with both. In the early stages of learning with cards you would ask their guides to influence the messages and guidance needed. The guides will see how they work with the cards and use this to build their link. We find it best if a medium works with the same set of cards as they learn to develop the readings. This is because it helps us learn to work with them, see how they interpret the cards and what they can pick up from their guides. They need to look at the cards as a whole and see what it makes them feel, then look deeper at symbols, colours and the energy the card gives out. They will find each card develops an individual meaning to them that we can then work with.

When the medium has built confidence with one set of cards, then we advise they try another, using their experience so far to expand their interpretation with the new cards. This expands the way they work. With some mediums we start to bring in awareness of loved ones in spirit, but this will vary depending on their ability and the way they are being taught.

With our medium friend, we found she connected to angel cards best, and being a creative visual person she used the pictures to build the reading. She used the same set for a while, and then we lead her to a second set of angel cards. We did also make odd words pop out to her on the cards to help with the messages we wanted to convey. As she developed, she started to feel clients' loved ones drawing near as she did card readings, as her mediumship connection was strengthening. With our guidance she used her judgment regarding whether or not to give the message. Then one day when she was at a mind and body fair, she was using the cards, and a client's granddad pushed forward and we asked him to tell her to ditch the cards. She asked her client if this was OK, and from that point on linked clairvoyantly to spirit without using the cards. Her confidence grew and she trusted us and she has only used the cards again when we have guided her to do so. We now feel they had served their purpose for her development.

We see readings with cards as a good stepping-stone on the development path of psychics and mediums. Depending on your individual personalities, some of you will progress from the cards easily, others will need the comfort of them as a prop for your trust. This is fine as all the messages will relate to what needs to be given the client at the time. We send people to the readers who will benefit from their style of reading and knowledge.

Now we would like to mention tarot cards too, which are decks of cards with pictures, symbols, words and numbers on them. Again the reader will use these cards as a tool for guidance in past, present and possible future outcomes. It takes a certain type of mind to use tarot cards and understand the messages they give. They act as an open book of philosophy and psychology; it helps you to see the deeper purpose in your lives and to understand human nature. Some people stay away from these cards as there is some belief amongst you they are evil. Remember there is no evil, only what your mind creates. As with all cards used in the correct way and intent, under the love and light umbrella, they will bring the guidance needed. As with all card decks the right one will be bought to you and call out to your heart. Our medium friend cannot use tarot cards; with her brain make up, dyslexia and number blindness they are not right for her. Remember you are all unique on life's journey so trust your intuition when something is right for you.

3. One card group circle exercise

Do this exercise in a circle. The teacher selects a pack of cards, just using the cards (not tarot for this). Ask each circle member to pick a card. Give them a few minutes to study the card, the picture, words and the energy they get from it. Now ask everyone to focus on the energy of the circle member to their right, and use the card to give a mini reading. Ask them one at a time to give their reading out loud for all to hear.

The point of this exercise is for them to gain confidence giving a message in front of other people. It also helps them interpret the card and energy under a bit of pressure, as they have to learn to let go of the anxious way they might feel. They need to learn to trust the messages they are receiving.

4. Psychometry exercise

Psychometry is the ability to gain impressions from objects belonging to people alive or dead by holding or touching them. This ability allows you to sense an object's history or obtain information about the person who owned the item. Remember everything is made of energy, and energy can record and absorb living physical vibration, including that person's energy. This method of development is used more for beginners. Some developed mediums might choose to carry on with objects to help with their readings and energy links.

As the teacher, advise your students to be patient as some will get amazing results immediately. Others may have to spend months achieving results, gradually developing their psychic abilities.

This is often practiced in pairs, reading an object another person has provided. This will allow them to test each other as well as encourage and congratulate each other as they make slow and steady progress. Also immediate feedback is important, so the student will learn quickly as they go.

Exercise: Sit down in a comfortable chair in a quiet space where you won't be disturbed. It's best to start with small objects that you can easily hold in your hands such as - handwritten letters or cards, a piece of jewelry, a watch, a key, or anything with some history of the person you are reading. Or it might be from a deceased loved one they are hoping to connect with. A recently purchased or acquired item is not a good choice, as it would not have had the chance to absorb the energy time line needed to read it.

For beginners, we suggest you close your eyes while doing

this exercise to help you focus. Pick up the item and hold it with both hands. Take note of any thoughts, images and feelings that come into your mind. Don't rush, stay focused and relaxed. Try not to interpret or analyse these psychic impressions, and try not to force them. After a few minutes, if you feel that you have not got any impressions then just try again another day with a different item. There's no pressure; imagine we're trying to find the key to unlock your mind, and some locks take longer to pick than others! In the initial stages of your development you may be more sensitive on some days more than others. Some objects may be able to hold stronger vibrations than others. Remember all the students are unique individuals, touching new energy for the first time – patience is key to teach at this stage.

5. Photograph reading

Ask your students to bring a photograph of a deceased loved one in a sealed envelope. Place on a table away from the circle to start with and provide paper and pen for them. After a meditation to help them all relax, invite them one by one to pick an envelope that is not theirs.

Now we split this exercise into two sections. You ask them to connect with their guides with the intent they bring forward the spirit energy of the loved one in the photograph.

For the first section of the exercise they need to keep the

envelope sealed, just holding it in their hand, writing down any images or words they receive. Give them five minutes for this.

In the second section of the exercise, let them open the envelope and study the picture, again writing down any information they receive. Give them 10 minutes for this.

If a student is struggling, ask them to look at the photograph and write down how it makes them feel. This often opens up their senses more and helps them to connect better.

At the end of the exercise ask each student one at a time to show their photograph so they know with whom they are connecting in the room. Then ask them to feed back what they got. Ask the recipient of the information to respond to the reader's information and give feedback.

Encourage and applaud each student, even a little achievement is a big step forward.

6. Historical place reading

This exercise will take a bit of planning on the teacher's part. First of all choose an old building with lots of interesting history and people associated with it. Research the history of the building, its use, and famous people associated with it, the décor and gardens. Include its owners up to the present day and its use now.

Run off one picture of the outside of the building for each student and a set of questions with spaces for answers.

There are a few question samples here for you – of course you can be creative and make up your own.

Write down any images or words that come into your head.

Name the building?
Year built?
Where is it?
Who was associated with the building over its history?
Was it ever sold, if so when and to whom?
What's it used for today?
Any names come to you?
Any other impressions come to you?

We suggest you allow the students 20 minutes for this exercise. When they are ready, ask them to come back into circle and individually ask them all to feed back on each question and go through one question at a time to the whole group, then the next question. Give them the answer after they have all answered each question. It is a bit of a suspense exercise for them and very enjoyable.

7. Written message exercise

This is the next step to inspiration writing with your guides. This exercise is to bring forward a written message from a loved one in spirit.

This can be done in pairs, and you provide pen and paper. Ask the students to sit opposite each other in silence, taking in each other's energies. Then ask them to ask for a loved one of the person opposite them to step forward and inspire a message.

Now, the result will depend on the student's capabilities. Ask them to write down if they feel a male or female, and who they might be, any details that come forward and a written message. Allow 15 minutes for this exercise. Help those who need a bit of support, giving guidance on how to connect and you should pick up on who is with them to help with this. But let them bring the message through themselves.

We don't want them to share their information yet, so just ask them all to rejoin the circle.

Ask the pairs to take in it turns to say what they felt as they connected, and what information they had and the message. If the other person cannot take the spirit details and description then ask other members if they recognise who it is.

It is interesting to observe, as the student might pick up on a spirit energy near them that's working with another student, or mix up the two, so be prepared for all scenarios.

Once, when watching our medium friend do this exercise, a new student to connecting with spirit picked up on a grandma and also a man in the family that had taken his own life. The student just had a jumble of information and could not interpret it yet, but had done what was asked and recorded what she had managed to pick up on. Our medium teacher connected with the two spirits who were with the student and could explain to the others so they understood, and divided up the information to help them. Now the way you teach is key, with encouragement and praise at all stages. If you help a student like this, it's key that they don't feel undermined. The new student did very well by getting so much information. As she progresses she will learn to ask more questions to spirit about her information and recognise two energies or more.

8. Mediumship connection exercise 1

This exercise is designed to help mediums develop and connect mind to mind to the spirit realm. It works with the teacher and the student working together as a team in a workshop or circle. The selected student will stand up at the front of the class with the teacher at their side. If it is a student in the early development stage ask them to shut their eyes and take a few deep-relaxing breaths. Set the intent with your student and – with both your guides that one spirit relative or friend for the group comes forward. Think of it as a square, teacher, teacher's guides, student and student guides all working together. All involved in this spiritual square will be building the energy to help the student make the connection. As the teacher, you will connect to the spirit the student brings forward, but not say anything unless we prompt you to do so.

Ask the student to tune into the energy coming forward from the spirit realm to connect with them. Give them a few minutes to tune in and feel the power build. Ask them if they feel spirit energy with them. If they say no, ask them to ask the spirit energy to draw as close as they can. Ask them to describe how they feel physically – they might feel, hot, cold, or other bodily sensations. Part of this learning is they have to feel the spirit energy with them and see them in their mind's eye. Then sense who they are, their personality, their sex, any physical traits and what they wish to come forth with in the message.

As they start, ask the student if they are drawn to anyone in the circle. Some students will be drawn to someone and others won't, remember every student and experience is unique to them. When the student names someone in the circle, ask the named person to speak and connect with what the student feeds out about their spirit connection. This is important, so there is a voice energy connection to and help the link. So now there are six involved the receiver of the message and their guides, all working as a team to make this happen.

As the confidence grows and the energy builds with your encouragement as the teacher, the student will have a better connection. We find this exercise works well if the teacher stands back and lets the student describe what's coming in from spirit, if we feel the student needs some help as the receiver is struggling to understand the information and saying no, no, we will give the teacher some information to help the connection. To keep this simple, for example, the spirit might have lived near a farm or we can give a simple memory link so the receiver can understand who the spirit is. When you start to hear yes, yes, the positive energy builds and strengthens the connection with the student.

We work this way with our medium friend, after gentle encouragement and giving the students a choice whether to stand up front of everyone and do this exercise. We witness all students do this exercise and connect with a loved one. Patience is needed by the teacher, and encouragement, making the student feel comfortable and not devalued if they don't do as well as their fellow students.

Part of the learning with this exercise is to make the student aware of the information they receive and the guides who are trying to work with them. For example is the spirit energy coming from left or right, does it vary with a male or female spirit? How do they know the spirit's sex, can they sense or see them. It's good for them to say this out loud in the early days, either giving a description as they go or explaining it after the exercise. Then next time they do a similar exercise they will recognise similar things happening again. Also encourage the student to ask spirit questions when the recipient of the message does not understand the evidence being given.

We feel in spirit that the student does not have to find five or six bits of evidence in robotic style, but one good piece of evidence that leaves no doubt who is with them or two, if there is still doubt in the receiver's mind. Once you have that strong yes, then you can give the message. Ask the student to trust what comes into their mind for the message, and the guidance needed for the recipient. Depending on their ability this could be a few words, or quite extensive information.

Whatever level the student achieves, always encourage and praise throughout the exercise. If they get something right, say that's wonderful, now see what else you can get. Keep this encouraging, positive environment in your teaching.

9. Mediumship connection exercise 2

You can build on the last exercise as the student's connection evolves.

You can pair up two students. One of them will take the lead to make the connection with the spirit loved one for a member in the circle. The second person is to link into the spirit once the connection is made.

The lead medium will start giving the evidence, allowing the second medium to say what they are picking up as well. Between the two, build a picture of the deceased person and connect with a receiver in the circle. The teacher needs to prompt and guide as necessary to help the student receive information. Depending on the time restraints of your circle, and how many people are present, they can swap with another pair. Make sure all students have a chance of being the lead medium.

To build on this exercise even further, suggest to the students they should go out and watch various mediums on platform, and as you watch, tune into spirit and see what you pick up. The student might even pick up things before the medium speaks them out loud. It is a good way to build connection and confidence.

We hope these exercises will help you all on your mediumship development path. Remember don't ever compare yourself to others. Teacher and student will always learn from each other, and students from other students. Remember you are all beautiful, unique individuals and do not let anyone steal that from you.

10. Developing signs, symbols and images

In this exercise we want to make the student think about how they connect to spirit, recognising how they create their messages.

This will be done through symbols, visions and feelings and mind-to-mind thought conversation.

In this exercise we want you concentrate on symbols. These can be for mother, father, grandmother, grandfather, heart attack, stroke, asthma, cancer, military career and so many more.

You will create a checklist for your student and this would be an on going exercise. As they develop their mediumship skills they can write down how they know these things. It takes time to build the signs with co-operation from the student and their guides. You can do a simple exercise where you ask the students to connect to their guide and ask for a symbol, word, image that would connect them with the spirit persons illness or career for example. Then as they practice giving messages, the guides would use these to help them.

The best way for us to describe this is to explain some signs we have developed with our medium friend.

For spirit that has served in the forces we created these signs:

Navy – The old cigarette packet with a Navy seaman on it

RAF – she is shown her father as he was in the RAF

Army – Camouflage uniform

For the first and second world wars:

First – a wooden cross

Second – a stone head stone and grave fields in France and Belgium

For illnesses the spirit might have had on earth:

Stroke or aneurysm – she gets a pain in her head

Heart attack - pain in arm or chest

Asthma – blue inhaler

Cancer – we help her sense this by showing her people that have passed in her own life of cancer

These are just a few basic samples for you. The students will all develop in their own way, with clairsentience, symbols and visions. Also remember as the students develop they will develop more of a KNOWING of these things and the symbols etc will no longer be used in some cases.

We find a check list is very important as a basis to start with. Create your own for your students and revisit the list often on their progression, to see how they are developing.

You are the teacher

The first breath teaches us about life
The first love is when you meet your soul
The first light takes away the darkness
The first step is the challenges we face
The first word is about the wisdom we seek
The first taste is about the choices we make
The first touch is the explorer inside us
The first look takes you to new horizons
The first teacher brings you knowledge
The first lesson brings you clarity of mind
The first child listens to your philosophy

You are the teacher

Section 7

Signs from the spirit realm

Spirit are around you all your life, from the moment the spirit within (soul) makes that first connection with the physical form, but many of you stay unaware of us as you live out your life's. Or if you see a glimpse into our realm, you pull away through the fear of the unknown. Many of your religions portray us as angels or evil as the devil, quite a contrast, this we understand, as we are just an unseen force you do not yet understand.

Over the centuries, most of you have had your pure love of spirit squashed, but in the last 20 years, a lot of you are stepping forward, not afraid to say you believe in the spirit realm. There are more light workers and positive vibrations on Mother Earth now, allowing us to make a better connection with you all. A great shift is occurring, slowly gaining in power, and our aim is to build on this to take you from the third dimension, stepping into the fourth, leading you to the fifth.

We have always given humanity signs to follow when we are asked for help, but often they are not seen by you. With your own energy shift, you will become more aware of them. Ask for your signs to come to you and try to be specific. But be aware when you have lost a loved one, because grief is a very strong emotion; it holds you to the past and stops you living in the present. You become so absorbed with these strong emotions that your heart closes to divine messages. We see grief stricken humans going to mediums for readings; they only want to hear from that one human they are grieving over. This affects their experience as they then block out all other spirit and messages that could help them. They want so desperately to hear from their loved ones, but they cannot see the signs their spirit guides or loved ones leave them. These feelings change with time; as their grief subsides, some will start to feel their loved ones near and will be comforted by this.

There are also the scientific ones amongst you that block us through their way of thinking, but again, when you have a strong sign you cannot ignore and cannot give any earthly explanation for, this can trigger you to grasp your spirituality and then break down the barriers. Due to humans blocking us through emotions or ego, we sometimes give our loving comforting messages to others close to them to pass on. When you receive a sign, it is a magical moment for you to experience in your lives, so try not to miss them. We have listed below some signs you can ask for or may experience when we are near.

The meaning of signs from the spirit realm

Feathers

Finding feathers is a sure sign spirit is around you, and one of the commonly known signs of the angels, guides and loved ones passed over. Feathers of any colour are a beautiful reminder that we are near, loving and supporting you from behind the scenes. When you find feathers in an unusual place, this is an especially powerful sign from the spirit realm.

We have used feathers as signs with our medium friend on her mediumship journey. We do a lot of connecting and channeling with her on dog walks and when she is out in nature, it's at these times she reflects with us and we often leave feathers on her path in front of her where she is going to walk. There was a time when she moved house, and we left grey and white feathers to reassure her. We would leave them at her front door, or places like her recycling bins where she would find them. She had quite a collection by the time she moved house. Another way we have used feathers is twice in the winter months left her feather patterns in ice on her car windows, both at times when she asked for a sign of reassurance from us.

White Feather - When you find white feathers, they're always a sign from your angels or loved ones in spirit … even when you're in a place where birds are present. They simply mean, *'I am around you, everything will be ok.'*

Black Feathers - Most often found during times of crisis or transition. Usually, you are already having problems and the black feather is a sign from spirit they are aware of your current life difficulties, and helping and supporting you. Ask us for guidance and watch out for more signs.

Yellow Feathers - The spirit realm is saying,

'Congratulations to you! Things are going well right now.' A positive sign for you to keep, and thank the spirit realm for the good things in your life.

Pink Feathers - A sign your spirit team and angels are joining in with the fun in your life and they will laugh with you but never at you. When you rejoice, we rejoice.

Blue Feathers - This colour is for protection and a time for calm and peace in your life. Find space in your life for serenity by taking a walk by water or meditating. You have to take the steps to make this calm in your life happen; ask us to help you make the space you need.

Red Feathers - Finding a feather with red on it means that we are helping with matters of the heart, and helping you to find passion and love in your life. We like to help you with your modern ways, for example a lot of you now use dating sites to seek love; when doing so you can ask us to guide you to the right person.

Green Feathers - This is a sign your guides and angels use to send you healing, and guidance to ensure you take good care of yourself spiritually and physically. A green feather can also indicate that it's time for you to slow down and concentrate on number one, YOU.

Grey Feathers - Your spirit team and angels are working behind the scenes on the problem that is worrying you. Be ready for our signs soon, watch out for our guidance, and be patient while we put things into place for you.

The meanings of feathers with different colour combinations

Black and white feathers represent protection, or the sense of a union. The contrast of the black and white shows you have some internal conflict over a problem at the moment; give all your worries to us and be kind to yourself.

Black mixed with purple represents a very deep spirituality. Your third eye is getting stronger, so work harder with us and all will become clear for your life's path.

Black, white and blue mixed feathers denote change on the horizon. The blue indicates we are placing protection and guidance around you to help with this transition period.

Brown and black is a sign you are achieving balance between the physical and the spiritual in your life.

Brown and white is for happiness, and a sign that you are being protected from harm. We are protecting your mental and physical well-being.

Feathers with red and green in them, or together, is a sign you are being assisted financially and we are bringing abundance to your life as a whole. This is a very lucky sign

Grey and white symbolise hope for you; there is

transition-taking place and your future is not set. You can make the changes needed with us walking beside you, ask us for guidance and more signs.

Coins

The human phrase 'pennies from heaven' does not mean we are showering you with money; it has become a common saying because coins, usually pennies, are often found in obscure places when you are thinking about loved ones. We like to use signs that we know you will recognise, and a small coin is easier for us to handle. The coins can have deeper meaning, so if you come across one, look at the date; does it having meaning for you? Always be assured, coins are deliberately placed on your path to show we are with you offering love, support and guidance.

We have left coins for our medium friend as signs, the one that stands out in her head is again when she was moving house and was clearing out her attic. Some of the items in the attic were from her husband's dead parents' house, so her thoughts were with them as they cleared those out. She had been sending thoughts out to his parents asking if they were doing the right thing in moving. While sorting boxes she found one single old photo album in a box that had pictures of a holiday they took in the late 1980s in Canada. She was happy to remember how healthy and well they were back then. Then she found some old video film; a couple of the clips were from that same holiday. Then at the end of the day, hidden behind all the boxes, she found a box she did not recognise, and she realised it was from her husband's parents' house. There was not much in it, just a couple of crystal vases and an old pickle tray. She put the glass dishes in the pickle tray and then tipped it upside down to see if it was marked metal on the base, and as she did this, we sent a coin, which fell onto the counter. It was a Canadian dollar! She realised she had had three signs from her in-laws telling her that everything would be OK.

Rainbows

We love using rainbows to make you pause and wonder at the beauty of Mother Earth. This is also a sign from the divine that we are with you. They are shown to you at times you need reassurance in your lives, and they offer you hope and comfort.

Last time we showed one to our medium friend was when she was doubting her spiritual journey after she moved house. She was driving over a bridge and wondered if she was doing the right thing staying connected with her old circle or would drift way. Then she saw a beautiful rainbow in the distance in front of her and knew it was the right thing to stay connected and all would be OK as we were with her.

Clouds

We do have fun using clouds as signs that we are near, and I'm sure you have seen earth images of the angel shapes we show you. We also use other images in the clouds that have meaning to you at that time. So look up to the sky, my friends, and while you are cloud gazing, be open to the images we send you.

Birds

We often use the robin as a sign from spirit, as it's a very popular bird amongst you and is often seen all year round in parts of your western world. They have a beautiful bird song that lifts the soul. Where there are no robins, we choose a bird of beauty that resonates with someone as a sign that spirit is near.

Our medium friend loves robins and we brought one to her in her new garden. She recently found out through another medium giving her a message that it was her uncle Robin in spirit bringing in the robin. We love using birds as signs and their bird song to lift your hearts.

Butterflies

These are such beautiful creatures that reflect the beauty of your world. We love to use butterflies as signs from the spirit realm as they signify transformation across many of your cultures on earth. The butterfly represents the inner spirit that has been released from the physical form. If you have been thinking of a loved one or asking for guidance, and a butterfly lands on you, or near you, know we are close and have heard your prayers.

Repetitive words, numbers and images

We give you lots of signs but we can also give verbal warnings, which may sound like a voice next to your ear or in your head. These are used to protect you on your life's path in the hope you heed us. With light workers, we also use signs such as repetitive words, numbers and images, because they have already acknowledged us and work with us; they are open to the signs and will be looking out for them. We do also use them with the rest of humanity, usually when we think you will see them; even if you don't understand it, it would be at a profound time in your life. These numbers are often shown to you three times or more. There are earth books written about these number sequences that have the meanings from spirit and their messages for you.

We have used angel numbers with our medium friend to help guide her. She has a book of angel numbers that she uses when she sees the signs. It is the same book she always refers to as we know the messages in it so can give her the right guidance. We have now given her a number 66, which is her own personal number from us as a reminder we are with her and all will be OK. This came about when we had guided her to open a spiritual centre and run spiritual services. She took hold of the challenge we had set her and made it happen trusting the journey. But the human ego let the doubt in asking if it was the right thing to do and she asked us for a sign. One night when driving home she had this thought in her head so we decided to send a sign, we sent three cars past her with 66 in the number plates. She saw the sign and understood and looked up the message in her angel number book. We chose this message, as she was worrying, being fearful which was affecting her hearing us. *'When you're burdened by worries, stress, or fear, it's more difficult to hear your angels' loving help. This is a message for you to spend time in prayer meditation. Ask for spiritual intervention, and open your arms to receive the help that always follows prayers.'* The night she opened her centre, she pulled out of her drive and saw a car parked opposite that was visiting her neighbour and had 66 in the number plate. This made her smile and off she went, confident she was doing the right thing. She still sees the number and trusts all will be OK.

Dreams

Spirit can use your dream state to give you guidance and show you your loved ones are OK after we have passed back to the spirit realm. When you sleep your vibration changes, your five senses slow down, and your sixth sense is given a chance to shine. You will find these dreams will be more vibrant than others and of course you will remember them. Some of you describe them as a waking dream, an experience you will rarely forget.

The gap between earthly reality and the spiritual realm changes during sleep and the fourth dimension is a dream state meeting place. This allows us to enter your mind, and your subconscious is open to ideas that your rational minds would not normally see or allow. We suggest you have a notebook by the bed, so you can remember any dreams and record ideas that come to you, they will change your life for the better.

Our medium has had many visits from passed loved ones and ascension beings in her dreams. Whenever one of her relatives or friends died we would send them to her in a dream to say they were OK, and it was interesting to observe that she did interact with them. She would also see them in the distance, but not be able to get through the veil to speak to them. One time we did this to help She make a connection to spirit was about nine years ago when her neighbour died of cancer. After a couple of weeks She dreamed she was looking at her neighbour sitting outside in a hot climate at a table, looking tanned and healthy. She asked him why he was there but he did not speak. She asked again and he laid down a card. When She read it, it said, 'Tell my wife I love her.' Afterwards, Sharon could not get this out of her mind, and eventually she gave his wife the message and his wife was very pleased to hear it. Our medium friend had hesitated, as she did not know how his wife would perceive this. If you receive a message in a dream, please pass it on, as we would not let you give anything out that is not needed. Even if the recipient seems unsure, you have done the right thing – be guided by the intuition that comes from your spirit soul within. Leaping forward in time, we are now using her dreams to introduce her star friends to her, an exciting time for us, I can tell you.

We also used her dreams to plant a seed of interest and to help our medium friend take notice of the spirit realm, we gave her a repetitive dream through her life, which she felt she had lived but was not of the modern age she was in. The dream was a glimpse of her time as spirit within with Marceline. In the dream, she would be visiting a black gravestone and vault, and also had glimpses of a large drawing room, a hall with lots of paintings and a bedroom she did not want to enter. She was led to a spiritual lady who was trained in past life regression and asked if she would have this experience with her, and she nervously agreed. This was the point we had been waiting for, as this past life regression sparked her interest in mediumship and the spirit realm. All of these dreams were our way of fuelling her imagination, energies and mind to help her on her spiritual journey, in the hope she took the right path.

Movement of objects

We do like to have a bit of fun, especially our young spirits, and move objects when you are not looking, then when you least expect it, the object will re-appear again. If you notice this happening and you do not like it, just ask us to stop and we will; this will tell us that you have at least seen our sign and are aware of your spirit friends. Or just ask us to return the object because you need it, it is all done in love and fun.

Scents

This is a very popular method for us to give signs that we are around you. It will be the scent of a favorite perfume, after shave or flower that a loved one liked while on earth. We also like to use tobacco and cooking smells associated with your loved ones too.

With our medium friend in her early days, we did give her smells, one was cigarette smoke when her sister in-law died of lung cancer from smoking. This was done to see what she could pick up and how it long it took her to associate it with spirit. So if you have a scent around you, see if it reminds you of anyone who has died – we might be testing you.

Temperature change

When spirit is near you and they come close to your energy to comfort you, you might experience a change in temperature; can be a coldness you feel or you might feel hot and flushed - this is all normal. It happens as we make contact with your energy field; the vibration from the spirit realm can slow or speed up the molecules in the air, resulting in a change in temperature. Every person will vary in how they react to our interaction with them. If you are in acceptance of this contact just go with it; if not, just ask us to stand back. You can always ask us to draw nearer when you are ready. Remember you are always in control.

As a medium you will experience various body temperature changes in your work with spirit. This is because your own energy field and physical body will react to our energies as we draw close. Everyone will be different and often as you get used to spirit this alters. Our medium friend usually gets hot when she works with spirit, she asks us to cool her down, which we try to do.

Music

Spirit love to use music for a sign or a message for you. You might hear a choir and not be sure where the singing comes from. You might be thinking about a passed loved one and their favorite song comes on the radio, or a song that had meaning around that person. If you hear a repeating song, listen to the words, ask spirit why you keep hearing it, and the first thing that comes into your head will be the answer.

Voices

Babies and animals have not yet taken on many of the filters, which can block your ability to clearly see your guides, angels or a member of your spirit family dropping in to say hello. Have you ever noticed a baby looking up smiling at what seems to you empty space? Or perhaps your pet's focus is captured by something you are unable to see; your dog's tail happily wagging at an unseen force. Yes, they are seeing and hearing our spirit realm. In the presence of their spirit team and spirit group visitors, babies, small children and animals will be at ease, showing signs of comfort and excitement.

We also use voice communication to adults to make them aware of spirit; quite often this is their first link to acknowledging us. It can sound like voices in the next room, or whispers; you cannot quite hear what they are saying, but when you reach the room it stops. Few of you are blessed with hearing us directly, like a person standing next to you; you will all mostly hear our thoughts in your head telepathically, as we draw into your energy field. But we would like to say as humanity ascends you would all hear us clearly one day.

Different coloured lights

Shafts of light streaming or shooting around you are definite indications of the spirit realm. Don't be afraid if you notice sparks of light or shadows around you. The digital technology you now use can capture orbs, signs that spirit energy is near you. Spirit don't want to harm you, this is normally a sign that they are trying to reach you directly. If you do not work with spirit and you think spirit are trying to contact you, seek out a recommended medium to see if they have a message for you.

Touch

We do like to draw close to your energy and touch your head, arms or hands to comfort you or give you healing. You might feel a tingle, or the sensation that something has just brushed your skin. This is a gentle touch of love and healing for you, it will give you comfort without you really knowing why.

On the mediumship journey you will come across a lot of these signs on your path. Also, when you give a message spirit will tell you of signs they have placed on your client's path as evidence they are near. As you work to connect with spirit the signs will become clearer to you, helping you on your spiritual path.

Signs from heaven

The beautiful butterfly on silent wing brings promises of life and wonderful things.

The promise of life and all things anew in a heavenly place veiled from you.

The rainbow shines in the darkened skies, bringing new hope when pain strikes.

Your tears that fall and never dry are wiped away with the colours in the sky.

The angels appear as fluffy white clouds to remind you of love to lighten your mood.

The white feather that lands at your feet is to help you to never admit defeat.

The coins that appear on your path are a reminder of our abundance of love.

The singing red breast robin is a friend to bring tunes to the heart that needs to mend.

These signs are from us with unconditional love; take them with you on your life's path.

Never forget we are a thought away to we meet in heaven again one day.

We wish you well on your mediumship journey

Remember, at the start of the book we said the journey of being a medium would come to those that had chosen this path, at different times on your life's timeline – a path chosen by you before your spirit came to Mother Earth.

The lessons you learn on your life's path will help you with your mediumship and giving caring, loving messages of those we sent to you, and you will have a deeper understanding of life. We guide who comes to you for readings and healing, using your experience and energy to help you give the reading that is needed for that person.

Key to this mediumship journey you are about to embark on is to TRUST. Trust your own first instincts and intuition as you walk your Earth's path and don't let your ego rule your head. We know everything we do in the love and light helps you make a step forward in helping guide you to reach your full potential as a medium and healer.

The change you will experience on this path will make you an awesome being. You will start the change of ascension bringing the divine light to you and others around you. Be the best you can be and be the teacher of kindness, love and light.

This book is the starting point, and a guidance handbook for you. There is so much to being a medium, but do not be overwhelmed – take it one step at a time. Do not compare yourselves to others as you are all unique and on your own journey. Support all fellow light workers, as you are all here to hold each other's hands as you work towards the ascension of humanity. You are all linked on your Mother Earth, supporting each other in spirit, so support each other on your human journey too.

Ask us for guidance and learn to read the signs we send to you. Study hard to gain the knowledge and wisdom needed to help you with your spiritual work. Together we will work as a team creating the best medium you can be.

Enjoy the journey my friend

Love, light and blessings x

Twilight years

As you reach your twilight years it is a time for human reflection.

You reflect on the pain in your life
You reflect on the shame in your life
You reflect on the anger in your life
You reflect on the moments you missed
You reflect on the moments of doubt
You reflect on the love of a child lost
You will reflect on lost love
You reflect on times of happiness
You reflect on what might have been
You reflect on life as a dream

But remember my friends this is all experiences of the human race. There should never be any thought of what if... I should have done this... if only...

What came about in your life was meant to be as it has been a pathway of learning and gaining knowledge.

As your twilight years end and you pass in to your life a new in the stars with us you will understand the journey that you took while on this Earth plane.

The Journey is for ascension, for a better way of being for humanity and for spirit self.

And if you wish my friend when you have reflected on your life on earth you may come back again and try to better the life you had before.

Or take the time to reflect further and try something new to enhance your growth while you are back with us in the spirit realm

Love and blessings

True happiness

Happiness comes from your inner core.
To find happiness look deep within your self.

Do you like what you see, how you behave?

Change the hate to love you have inside you
Change the negativity to positivity around you

Open your eyes to your world and beyond
Open your eyes and find your soul.

Your true self lies within you waiting
A hand of friendship is being extended

Take the love that goes with this gesture
Hold it close to your heart and breath

Now this is the start of your happiness
Go forward with your new inner flame

Go forward and shine bright and extend
to others the Friendship hand of light

NOTES

NOTES

NOTES

NOTES

NOTES

NOTES

NOTES

NOTES

ABOUT THE AUTHOR

Sharon Bengalrose is a medium and holistic healer based in Newport, South Wales (UK). Through her work with spirit, she loves to help people find happiness and heal, raising their positive energy levels with messages from loved ones in spirit. Also to teach others about the spiritual path and mediumship.

Her fifth book, **'Step into the Mind of a Medium**, follows on from her previous books, 'Utopia', 'The Magic of Spirit', The Magic of Words', Ayderline the Spirit Within' and 'Inspiration Guidance Cards'. Sharon's books are available on Amazon, as well as her own website www.bengalrose.co.uk.

Visit her website www.bengalrose.co.uk to find out more about Sharon. You will also find her on twitter @SBengalrose and FaceBook Bengalrosehealing.

Sharon has a YouTube channel with over one hundred spiritual guidance videos search 'Sharon Bengalrose'.

Sharon also welcomes contact through email Sharon@bengalrose.co.uk

Made in the USA
Lexington, KY
16 May 2018